Thailand

To reach a better understanding of Thailand means getting to grips with the concept of Thainess, the ethnocentric ideology that went hand in hand with the development of the modern Thai nation throughout the 20th century, and echoes of which are still very much in evidence. In fact, if you look closely, the causes of many of the divisions that agitate contemporary Thai society – some more apparent, others simmering beneath the surface – can be traced back to the desire to create a single hegemonic culture in a multi-ethnic country, something often imposed through violently enforced Thaification. From the north, where prejudice against the Isan people persists, to the south, where the separatist desires of the majority-Malay and Muslim provinces are repressed through draconian special laws, the conflict between the centre (Bangkok) and the periphery is a wound that has never healed – not only in terms of geography but also in the hierarchy and the centralisation of power, as, for example, in the religious sphere where the state attempts, often in vain, to tame the unofficial strands of Buddhism. The large street demonstrations of recent years and the twists and turns (and coups) of the political establishment are underpinned by similar dynamics: the tensions between those on the margins of society, or members of an emerging class that still lacks a voice, and the conservative, aristocratic and entrepreneurial elite close to the centre of power. If Thailand wants to break away from its limiting role as a popular tourist destination, capitalise on its economic weight and project its soft power around the world, it must learn from the courage and critical spirit of this new generation with its belief in freedom and civil rights. It could even be argued that it is precisely this anti-democratic prevarication that is the most *un*-Thai characteristic of all, in a society that also has a sunny side, built on harmonious coexistence, kindness, being inclusive of ethnic minorities and refugees and (relative) tolerance towards the LGBTQ+ community. Try as those in power might to impose a single culture, ethnicity and religion, the real Thai strength seems to lie elsewhere, in syncretism and assimilation.

Contents

Some Numbers	6
The Song: 'Bangkok Legacy' — Prabda Yoon	8
'Expecto Patronum' — Claudio Sopranzetti	11
A look at the bizarre struggle between democratic forces and monarchism in Thailand.	
Becoming Bangkokian: How to Be a Hyphen-Thai — Philip Cornwel-Smith	31
Thai identity and that of Bangkok are often conflated, even by the capital's inhabitants themselves. So what makes you a Bangkokian? And what distinguishes a Thai from a foreigner living in this metropolis in the heart of Asia?	
Higher Powers — Pitchaya Sudbanthad	47
A land of countless religious beliefs, for centuries Thailand has seen Buddhism intertwined with the power of the state. But, however hard the powers that be try to tame and centralise the religion, the authorities struggle to control the everyday practices of millions of people and traditions that depart from the 'official' school.	
Generational Trauma in Thailand's Deep South — Veerapong Soontornchattrawat	63
In the three Malay-majority provinces in the South the civilian population finds itself at the mercy of armed separatist groups as well as central government. Reporting from the heart of Pattani province, a journalist meets some of the people who are trying to stop the cycle of violence.	
Heartland — Peera Songkünnatham	85
Off the tourist trails and often looked down upon by Bangkok, every so often Thailand's Northeast comes back into fashion. From K-pop to MasterChef, everyone is talking about Isan just now, but the story told from outside is one steeped in nostalgia and stubborn stereotypes.	
The Bodiless Woman and Other Ghost Stories — Emma Larkin	99
You're never far from a ghost in Thailand – often, although not always, malevolent. Rather than asking whether they are real or not, it is wise to placate them with prayers and offerings.	

Add a Pinch of Coriander — Valeria Palermi — 119

Taking its cue from Japan and South Korea, the Thai establishment is focusing on soft power to boost the nation's international prestige and its economy. Often, however, its measures are timid and fail to go far enough to stimulate a debate and bolster a cultural ecosystem in which freedom of thought and speech are still on shaky ground.

A Country With No Refugees — Nicha Wachpanich — 133

In a country where refugees officially do not exist, a flood of exiles, primarily from Myanmar, are finding refuge from persecution. But with its chauvinistic policies, bureaucratic absurdities and shortage of labour, Thailand has an ambiguous attitude to immigration.

There Has Been Blood — Diana Hubbell — 149

The global thirst for palm oil has never been more ravenous. Caught in a stranglehold between the industry's needs and a multigenerational war waged on Thailand's poor, the farmers of some communities in the south of the country have banded together to defend their land rights.

Boys' Love — Jidanun Lueangpiansamut — 171

In one of the Asian countries most open to LGBTQ+ themes, the Japanese literary genre of *yaoi* has flourished, with its love stories featuring gay men and aimed at an audience mainly comprised of young heterosexual women. But, in spite of the global success of Thai TV series based on these books, many questions still remain over the way LGBTQ+ people's lives are represented.

Ethnotourism — Andrea Staid — 184
The Playlist — 'Ted' Yuthana Boonorm — 188
Digging Deeper — 190

The photographs in this issue were taken by the independent Thai photojournalist **Jittrapon Kaicome**, who works with NGOs and international publications and whose projects focus on the countries of the Mekong region. Since 2014 he has been telling stories about his native city, Chiang Mai, during Northern Thailand's air pollution crisis, a topic that awakened his interest in the climate crisis. Having grown up in a multi-ethnic society, he feels the need to raise public awareness of the region's underrepresented ethnic communities. He has also documented the regions of Thailand that border Laos and Myanmar, which are defined by the Mekong and Salween rivers.

Some Numbers

AN UPPER-MIDDLE-INCOME COUNTRY

GDP per capita in selected Asian countries at purchasing power parity, 2024, international $

Country	
Taiwan	76,860
Japan	54,180
Malaysia	39,300
China	25,020
Thailand	**23,400**
Indonesia	16,860
Vietnam	15,470
Philippines	12,190
Laos	10,240
India	10,120
Cambodia	8,290
Myanmar	5,200

SOURCE: FMI

THE HAPPY FEW

Share of national wealth held by the richest 1%, selected countries, 2022

Country	%
South Africa	54.9
Chile	49.8
Brazil	48.7
Russia	47.6
Thailand	**47.5**
USA	34.9
China	32.6
Italy	22.1
UK	21.1
Netherlands	13.2

SOURCE: WORLD INEQUALITY DATABASE

OUT OF POVERTY ...

% of the population living below the national poverty line (calculated, in 2020, at 2,762 baht (c. $80) per person per month)

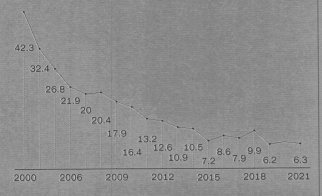

SOURCE: OURWORLDINDATA.ORG

... BUT INCREASINGLY IN DEBT

Countries with the highest household debt, % of GDP, 2024

	Country	%
1	Switzerland	128.3
2	Australia	111.8
3	South Korea	105.1
4	Canada	102.4
5	Hong Kong	95.8
6	Netherlands	94.9
7	New Zealand	94.5
8	Sweden	88.2
9	**Thailand**	**86.9**
10	Denmark	86.2
11	UK	83.2

SOURCE: FMI

ROYAL WEALTH

The world's richest monarchs, 2024, estimated net worth in billions of $

Thailand 43	Brunei 28	Saudi Arabia 18
King Vajiralongkorn	Sultan Hassanal Bolkiah	King Salman bin Abdulaziz Al Saud
Abu Dhabi 18	Dubai 14	Luxembourg 4
Sheikh Mohammed bin Zayed Al Nahyan	Sheikh Mohammed bin Rashid Al Maktoum	Grand Duke Henri

SOURCE: VISUAL CAPITALIST

ONE NIGHT IN BANGKOK

The world's most visited cities, 2023 (in millions). Before the Covid-19 pandemic Bangkok was regularly in the top 3.

1	Istanbul (Turkey)	20.2
2	London (UK)	18.8
3	Dubai (UAE)	16.8
7	**Bangkok (Thailand)**	**12.2**

SOURCE: EUROMONITOR

RICE KINGDOM

Major rice-exporting countries, 2023–4, thousands of tonnes

① India – 16.5
② **Thailand – 8.2**
③ Vietnam – 7.6
④ Pakistan – 5.0
⑤ USA – 2.6
⑥ China – 2.2
⑦ Cambodia – 1.9
⑧ Myanmar – 1.8

SOURCE: STATISTA

KEEPING BUSY

< 2%

unemployment rate since 2002 with a record low of 0.3% in 2013; this is low even by the standards of the region

SOURCE: WORLD BANK

ARTICLE 112

272

people prosecuted for the offence of *lèse-majesté* between July 2020 and April 2024; in the same period approximately 2,000 individuals were brought to trial for political offences of various kinds

SOURCE: TLHR

SINOPHILES

Perception of China in the Indo-Pacific region, % of respondents

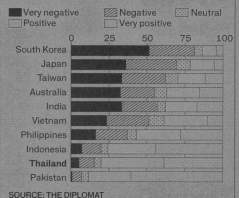

SOURCE: THE DIPLOMAT

SINO-THAI

Chinese communities worldwide, 2022, millions; figures include all those who identify as Chinese

SOURCE: STATISTA

Some Numbers

The Song: 'Bangkok Legacy'

PRABDA YOON

Hip-hop entered the mainstream of Thai music in the mid-1990s, thanks to the humorous and catchy tunes by such pioneering artists as Joey Boy and the angst-ridden trio Thaitanium. Musically, early Thai hip-hop was close enough to the works of the American rappers they aspired to emulate, but, because most of the artists were from privileged backgrounds, what they rapped about tended to focus largely on relationships and domestic bourgeois problems. It was pop music in the style of rap. Its popularity was limited to urban, mostly Bangkok, middle-class youth. Apart from the use of explicit language and sexual innuendo, it was neither revolutionary nor disruptive. It was party music for cool city kids.

Things changed when the allure of hip-hop culture reached the working class, thanks, no doubt, to widespread access to the internet. Aspiring artists started to rap about their struggles, question their conditions, voice their frustrations, and, by using social media for exposure, they no longer had to worry about censorship.

Youngohm (Ratthaphong Phoorisit) belongs to this new generation of Thai rappers. He was attending a Bangkok temple school when he started, competing in rap battles and eventually becoming a hip-hop sensation with many millions of views on YouTube, all while still in his late teens. His first hits, released between 2017 and 2018, were slow songs about heartbreak and his self-made success, typical subject matter in popular

PRABDA YOON is a Thai writer and film-maker based in Bangkok.

Thai hip-hop of the time. Youngohm had exceptional writing skills, especially the way he was able to blend Thai vernacular with English, street talk with poetry.

'Bangkok Legacy' is the title song from Youngohm's first full-length album. It came out in 2020 during the most intense period of the pandemic. It was also a politically turbulent time for Thailand, one of the critical turning points in its recent history. The government of the day was under military control, and the prime minister was Prayut Chan-o-cha, the ex-army general who staged a coup and seized power from a democratically elected government in 2014. Long-simmering anti-dictatorship sentiments and anger at the government's mismanagement of the pandemic combined and exploded in widespread street protests in Bangkok, predominantly by crowds of young people from all backgrounds. It was also the first time in recent memory that the untouchable monarchy was challenged.

Of course, not all Thais approved of the uprising. Right wingers and conservatives accused the protesters of being brainwashed by Western media, and most people in the privileged classes went about as if nothing was happening. The majority of mainstream artists would not dare to stick their necks out, and they continued to offer escapism to the public. By this time Youngohm was already famous. He was doing good business, getting product endorsements and making super-viral music and videos. To put out a song like 'Bangkok Legacy' would be a huge risk to his career. He did exactly that.

The song opens with a question to the ruling power: 'Are you all doing well, sirs? With the money you get through corruption? I don't see any damn dog coming out to admit it. I reckon we're from different classes, maybe people like me aren't even human?' The beat is infectious, but it's clear from the off that this ain't party music. In the second verse Youngohm introduces Bangkok as a city of either good or evil 'depending on how you see it', a city that can offer either happiness or suffering 'depending on whether you got gold, otherwise you might not survive it'. The words become even more daring, calling out the prime minister and deputy prime minister (also an ex-general) at the time by name and referring to the military crackdowns in 2010 in which eighty-seven people died and many went missing.

'Sorry to be a rebel,' opens the song's final verse. 'But everyone in this society is all the same, if I don't change when is it going to be over?' Youngohm then ends with the question 'When will Bangkok ever find peace?' That question has yet to be answered. Many key leaders of the 2020 protests are now in prison. The ruling power still runs the show. For many visitors Bangkok may be packed with cheap fun, great food and friendly faces, but for the natives who value fairness and justice it is also a cruel and corrupt city.

'Bangkok Legacy' may be a topical song, a song that invokes a moment in time in this city full of contradictions, but the fact that it comes from someone like Youngohm makes it special. He is young (now just twenty-six), talented and is liked by the mainstream. Most people like him would not dare write a song like 'Bangkok Legacy' even if they wanted to. His courage is inspiring and truly hip-hop. I consider it a quintessential Bangkok song because the fact that this city can produce someone like Youngohm gives me hope.

'Expecto Patronum'

CLAUDIO SOPRANZETTI
Translated by Eleanor Chapman

May 2024: a Red Shirt demonstrator raises his hand in a three-finger salute during a memorial rally to honour the ninety-plus dead and 2,100 injured following the Thai military's crackdown on the United Front for Democracy Against Dictatorship (UDD) protests at Phan Fa Lilat Bridge and Ratchaprasong in April and May 2010. The three-finger gesture, like many other symbols used during Thai protests, is a pop reference and is taken from *The Hunger Games*.

A look at the bizarre struggle between democratic forces and monarchism in Thailand.

Halfway up Ratchadamnoen Road, the vast Parisian-style boulevard that links the Grand Palace and the Thai parliament, the Democracy Monument stands alone in the middle of an enormous roundabout.

Commissioned in 1939 by Plaek Phibunsongkhram, the military dictator at the time, to commemorate the 1932 revolution that had put an end to absolute monarchy, the monument encapsulates the profound contradictions of Thailand's democratic history. It was designed by the Thai architect Chitrasen Aphaiwong and sculpted by Corrado Feroci – an Italian artist almost unknown in his own country who had risen to prominence in Thailand and would later be acclaimed as one of the fathers of modern Thai art. At the centre of their creation stands a huge statue of a palm-leaf manuscript representing the country's first constitution, introduced by the post-revolutionary government. Guarding it, but also arguably looming over it, are four imposing, wing-like structures representing the four branches of the armed forces (the army, the police, the navy and the air force) that took part in the 1932 revolution, or *coup d'état*, depending which side you were on. The relief sculptures at the base of the wings portray them as personifications of the will and values of the nation, guardians of the constitution and champions of democracy.

A statue of the constitution encircled by monuments to the same armed forces that since 1932 have torn it up thirteen times through military coups might seem utterly bizarre, and yet this is just the first of many peculiarities colouring recent Thai political history. What you are about to read is, in fact, a story full of contradictions, where seemingly incongruous symbols and references seem to blend into one, preposterous moments take on epochal significance and comedic events turn out to be deadly serious.

This is the story of Anon Nampa, a forty-year-old lawyer, activist, poet – one of Thailand's best legal minds – who, at the time of writing, finds himself in Block 4 of Bangkok Remand Prison. There he is serving a ten-year sentence and awaiting another fourteen trials for various crimes, from using an amplifier without permission to twelve charges of *lèse-majesté*, each of which could potentially cost him three to fifteen years' imprisonment. The most serious of these accusations, for which he is still awaiting a verdict, is for having dressed up as Harry Potter and broken one of the taboos of J.K. Rowling's fantasy world

CLAUDIO SOPRANZETTI is an anthropologist and associate professor at the Central European University and Quondam Fellow at All Souls College, Oxford. He is the author of *Red Journeys: Inside the Thai Red-Shirt Movement* (2012), *Owners of the Map: Motorcycle Taxi Drivers, Mobility and Politics in Bangkok* (2017) and, together with Sara Fabbri and Chiara Natalucci, of the graphic novel *The King of Bangkok* (2021).

and modern-day Thailand alike: publicly speaking the name of the principal villain, 'He-Who-Must-Not-Be-Named'.

More broadly, this is the story of contemporary Thailand, a country that for years now has been caught in a never-ending spiral of political openings and repressive crackdowns, mass movements followed by *coups d'état*, constitutions written only to be torn up, election results ignored and winning parties dissolved by national courts. A country that, especially since King Vajiralongkorn ascended the throne in 2016, walks a tightrope between honest discussions about the future of the monarchy and attempts to stifle any debate and return the institution to the glorious absolute sovereignty it lost in 1932.

*

But let's return to the Democracy Monument and its history.

Largely left alone in the decades following its construction, in 1973 it became the focus of a popular uprising against yet another military regime, a period of political conflict with glimpses of democracy to which the armed forces violently put an end in 1976. Although the military were triumphant this time, too, the Italian sculptor's work became a powerful symbol for Thai democratic struggles. The monument was the site of the 1992 mass protests that ended the long line of military dictatorships. There again, in 2009, the Red Shirts – a movement formed in opposition to the 2006 military coup that had deposed the elected prime minister, Thaksin Shinawatra – held their first protests before bringing the whole of Bangkok to a standstill the following year and then pushing for new elections in 2011. And, once again, in July 2020 the monument became the stage for the latest wave of protests, this time led by a group of students and activists organising under the name Free Youth.

This movement had emerged during the Covid-19 pandemic to oppose the military government of General Prayut Chan-o-cha, who had staged the 2014 *coup d'état*. After taking power the general had enacted a new constitution that made a civil government almost impossible and, after the 2019 elections, allowed the military to form a government with less than 25 per cent of the vote. As if this wasn't enough, in 2020 the new government used the Constitutional Court to dissolve the Future Forward Party, a progressive political party that had emerged in 2018 as the most vocal parliamentary critic of General Prayut, becoming just the latest in a long line of democratic parties falling victim to military power and the connivance of national courts.

To protest against all of this, on 3 August 2020 the Free Youth movement assembled for a rally with a title that was intriguing, to say the least: 'Harry Potter vs. You-Know-Who or He-Who-Must-Not-Be-Named'. While their predecessors had crowded around the Democracy Monument brandishing placards and flags, these protesters wore black cloaks and held magic wands.

This came after an earlier protest on 18 July when a small group, mostly made up of students, had taken to the streets in breach of lockdown restrictions to call for the dissolution of the military-dominated parliament, demand a new constitution and an end to intimidation of political opponents. This time, however, the protest seemed to be headed in a different direction. On a small stage erected beside the Democracy

YELLOWS AND REDS

The last two decades of Thailand's political history are often presented as a battle between two elites, but this narrative overlooks two grassroots movements that, especially in the period between the two *coups d'état* of 2006 and 2014, shaped a political conflict that still reverberates to this day. The Yellow Shirts – the People's Alliance for Democracy (PAD) – emerged in opposition to Thaksin Shinawatra's government. Accusing the former prime minister of corruption and anti-monarchist tendencies, the Yellow Shirts organised protests calling for royal intervention to remove him from power, a new constitution and a replacement to the one-person, one-vote electoral system that they believed favoured the wrong leaders. Despite being in the minority, the movement achieved its goal with a military coup on 19 September 2006. This led to the formation of the Red Shirts – the United Front for Democracy Against Dictatorship (UDD). Initially comprised mostly of Thaksin's supporters, the movement subsequently spread, especially in the provinces of the Northern and Northeastern regions, to encompass various democratic networks, human rights activists, critics of the monarchy and other key progressive figures. In 2008 a party aligned with Thaksin and the Red Shirts won the elections, but the result was overturned by the Constitutional Court. The following year the Red Shirts organised the biggest protests in the country's history, culminating in an occupation of the centre of Bangkok between March and May 2010. The military intervened, killing almost a hundred demonstrators. The government fell a few months later, and the new elections were won by a party led by Thaksin's sister, Yingluck Shinawatra. In 2013, concerned about the Shinawatra family's return to power, the Yellow Shirts barricaded Bangkok and occupied government buildings. Under the pretext of putting an end to political instability, the armed forces took control on 22 May 2014, marking the start of a new phase of authoritarian rule that persists to this day. (C.S.)

Monument, a scarecrow wrapped in a black cloak with a printout of the face of Ralph Fiennes as Lord Voldemort, Harry Potter's nemesis, pinned to it, stood before a huddle of protesters bearing magic wands and placards reading 'I'm not scared of you' and 'Exiles are people too'. Hanging beneath the stage, a purple banner with gold lettering bore the protest's slogan: 'Cast a spell to banish You-Know-Who'. Around the neck of the scarecrow dangled a photo of Voldemort in an ornate frame, a not-so-veiled reference to the portraits of the king that adorn public spaces in Thailand.

'Harry Potter is the story of young wizards and witches and their teachers fighting against the forces of evil, whose name no one dares to speak, who are trying to take over the kingdom,' Thatchapong Kaedam, one of the protest's young leaders, declares from the stage. 'Fighting the network of You-Know-Who is the hardest thing.'

The crowd murmurs in approval.

'The network of You-Know-Who,' Thatchapong continues, 'has infiltrated almost all institutions, all organisations,

Top: Holding tight to balloons being tugged by the wind in front of a portrait of King Vajiralongkorn (regnal name Rama X) and his queen at an intersection in Yasothon province.
Bottom: Royal guards in front of the Grand Palace in Bangkok.

Top: Political activist Panusaya Sithijirawattanakul, aka Rung, giving a speech in Bangkok in May 2024. She demanded justice for the Red Shirt protesters who died in the military crackdown and for her friend Netiporn Sanesangkhom, who was jailed and died in prison while on hunger strike to demand reform to the justice system and an end to the imprisonment of political dissidents.
Bottom: An exhibition in Bangkok, organised by the Move Forward Party, highlighting the circumstances of jailed political activists. In the centre is a cut-out of lawyer Anon Nampa.

in the human and wizarding world alike. It's even taken control of the Ministry of Magic.'

More agreement from the crowd.

'But ever since Prayut Chan-o-cha came to power ...' He pretends to falter. 'Hold on, what's Prayut doing in this book? Forget Prayut ... Since a new minister of magic, a puppet of You-Know-Who, came to power, do you know who started to see things differently? Young witches and wizards, young people like us. So take up your wands, and let's fight Voldemort and his network.' Thatchapong bellows for the crowd to turn, wands aloft, towards the Democracy Monument.

'Expecto patronum!' the protesters chant, appropriating a spell from the Harry Potter universe that uses happy memories to conjure up a guardian animal. 'I want everyone to think of Wanchalearm's smile. [A reference to Wanchalearm Satsaksit, a young activist who had disappeared while in exile a few months earlier.] Think of the smiles of our friends who have been forced into exile. Think of the smiles of our friends who were abducted and disappeared because they think differently, and point your wand into the sky,' Thatchapong concludes.

In Thailand, the use of symbols and codewords to speak about the monarchy has a long history. Even though the references are widely understood, such allusions are essential for expressing criticism while maintaining plausible deniability and protecting oneself against accusations of *lèse-majesté*. These codewords, however, have to be continually reinvented, which, for those not in the know, can become problematic.

I can still remember how confused I was during one of my earliest stays in the country, when a conversation criticising the then sovereign hastily ended with the phrase 'you must really want a pizza ...' followed by much laughter. It took me weeks to understand that pizza – in particular, the Pizza Company, whose freephone number was 1112 – was a codeword for the *lèse-majesté* law, Section 112 of the Thai Criminal Code. Somewhat convoluted, I thought, but then again, the whole point of a code is to be hard to decipher and never completely public.

And yet, on that small stage next to the Democracy Monument, on 3 August the code was publicly deciphered, at first apprehensively but then with no hesitation. After several poems and songs, the microphone passed to the only protester dressed up as Harry Potter himself: Anon Nampa, a plump thirty-six-year-old lawyer with a high forehead, round glasses and a mop of hair in a side-parting. Bundled up in a red-and-gold striped Gryffindor scarf, he swapped his wand for the microphone and started with a bang.

'It is of the utmost importance that we speak openly about how the monarchy is involved in Thai politics. We must accept the truth: part of the reason that the students and the people are protesting is that many want to ask questions about our monarchy.'

All of a sudden silence falls. The crowd is dumbstruck.

'At demonstrations we speak in code, but none of what we say can refer to anyone other than our monarch ... Right now we are facing a hugely important problem: our monarchy has moved further and further away from democracy ...'

The entire crowd seems to be holding its breath.

Call 112
A new generation of activists

Claudio Sopranzetti

Parit Chiwarak
aka: Penguin

BORN: 1998, in the Ko Kha district of Northern Thailand. Son of a local accountant, he moved to Bangkok as a child.
EDUCATION: Graduated from the prestigious Triam Udom Suska School then studied political sciences at Thammasat University in Bangkok.
ACTIVISM: At the age of just sixteen, as general secretary of the Education for the Liberation of Siam group, he unfurled a banner before Prayut Chan-o-cha, criticising the corrupt military junta. In the years that followed he kept up his social criticism and started to rack up charges for his activism at protests and online. He was one of the leaders of the 2020 student protests and one of the most vocal critics of the monarchy. He was the first to be arrested after the demonstration on 10 August, was released on bail and then, along with Rung, arrested again on 15 October on a charge of sedition. Between 2020 and 2024 Penguin was in and out of prison awaiting final judgements.
LÈSE-MAJESTÉ CHARGES: In addition to the first charge, received alongside Rung on 25 November 2020, he faces another twenty-four, an unprecedented number in Thailand. In July 2024 he received his first sentence of two years' detention. If found guilty of all charges, he could be sentenced to up to 375 years.

Jatupat Boonpattararaksa
aka: Pai Dao Din

BORN: 1991, in Chaiyaphum, Isan. Son of a Bangkok lawyer who moved to Northeastern Thailand to follow cases of local activists who were victims of repression, violence and assassination.
EDUCATION: Following in his father's footsteps, he studied law at Khon Kaen University. He graduated in 2017 while detained in the city jail.

ACTIVISM: He rose to national fame in 2013 when, with a group of students – the Dao Din group – he participated in anti-mining protests in the town of Loei. After the 2014 coup he founded the New Democracy Movement (NDM) in opposition to Prayut Chan-o-cha's military dictatorship. He was arrested for the first time following a peaceful protest in the presence of the general and

then again for distributing flyers criticising the new draft charter that was being put to referendum. He went on hunger strike in prison, making him famous among young Thai activists.
LÈSE-MAJESTÉ CHARGES: On 3 December 2016 he was accused of *lèse-majesté* for sharing a BBC Thailand biography of the king on Facebook, the first *lèse-majesté* case since Vajiralongkorn ascended the throne. In August 2017 he was sentenced to two years and six months in prison before being released on 10 May 2019 following a royal pardon. After participating in the 2020 protests and demanding reform to the monarchy, Pai was accused of *lèse-majesté* yet again and, in September 2024, given another three years. He is currently in jail, continuing his activism while awaiting the outcome of a bail request.

Panusaya Sithijirawattanakul
aka: Rung

BORN: 1998, in Nonthaburi, a small city north of Bangkok, the third and youngest daughter of a middle-class family who own a garage.
EDUCATION: Studied sociology and anthropology at Thammasat University in Bangkok.
ACTIVISM: After enrolling at university she became more involved in student politics, becoming the spokesperson of the Students' Union. In 2020 she protested against the dissolution of the Future Forward Party. On 10 August 2020 she rose to national fame as the face of a new generation of activists openly critical of the crown by reading out the ten demands for reform of the monarchy. She was arrested on 15 October 2020 on a charge of sedition and released on bail sixteen days later to await trial. This would be the first of many imprisonments.
LÈSE-MAJESTÉ CHARGES: On 25 November 2020 she was charged, along with eleven other activists, for their calls for reform to the monarchy. Nine other charges followed. If found guilty she could face up to 150 years in prison.

> '**If something happens because I told the truth, if I am threatened, persecuted or killed, I will not regret it. Today I told the truth, and this truth will be with each and every one of you, brothers and sisters.**'

'Don't leave the marginalised to have to talk about the monarchy and then face threats and harassment alone. Don't leave it to the political exiles to be the ones to talk about the monarchy only to be brutally murdered and disappeared. As of now this cannot continue.'

Some isolated applause.

'I'm not just talking for the sake of talking. I have suggestions for addressing these problems. We have to amend those sections of the constitution that concern the monarchy,' Anon continues before embarking on a fifteen-minute description of legal details about which sections need amending and which taxes the monarch has dodged, discussing constitutional law and what it means to be a democracy with a king as the head of state, as if he has forgotten about the bizarre costume he is wearing. 'Today Harry Potter is forced to talk about these things.' The crowd is revived, bursting into cathartic applause.

'From this moment on, if those who invite me to speak ask me to wriggle and avoid mentioning the monarchy, I will not ... If something happens because I told the truth, if I am threatened, persecuted or killed, I will not regret it. Today I told the truth, and this truth will be with each and every one of you, brothers and sisters. Let's fight the dictators until we all live in a real democracy.'

The crowd erupts, holding their wands up to the sky.

It might be difficult for someone unfamiliar with Thailand to understand how powerful and stirring those words were, and why would anyone dress up as Harry Potter to utter them. But hidden under that black cloak was one of the country's most serious and respected critics.

Born into a farming family in 1984 in Thung Khao Luang, a village in the Roi Et province in the country's northeast, Anon first became involved in politics at school. His participation in protests against the privileges and favouritism enjoyed by wealthier students and his calls for the school to be opened up to female students earned him the school council presidency and the nickname the Little Communist. In 2002 Anon, as many young people from the northeast of Thailand do, moved to Bangkok, initially to study sociology and anthropology and then, after a few months, law.

In 2006, after Anon graduated, two events changed his life. First, a military coup deposed Thaksin Shinawatra, the first widely popular prime minister of Thailand, prompting Anon's interest in national politics. Then, like all Thai men, he had to face the lottery for military service. He drew a red card and so was forced to enlist, suddenly finding himself among the ranks of the same armed forces he had been protesting against. But this year of military service did not go to waste. Before it was over Anon passed the bar exam and won his first case in military court, defending

THAKSIN SHINAWATRA

Born in 1949 in Chiang Mai to a wealthy family of Chinese origin, Thaksin joined the police in 1973 and left at the end of the 1980s. Using his contacts in the police and the military, in the following decade he launched a computer renting business, then a private television channel and finally the largest mobile-phone network in Thailand. In 1994 he entered politics as foreign minister. In 1998, in the wake of a severe economic crisis in Southeast Asia, he founded the Thai Rak Thai Party, which won elections in 2001 and 2005, making him the first Thai prime minister to last a full parliamentary term. A good salesman, Thaksin understood that satisfying his voters' desires for consumerism and political representation would provide the foundation of his power, and he achieved unprecedented electoral support by creating an economic model that offered market liberalisation for the upper classes and an expansion of social welfare for poorer citizens. In 2006 the crown and the military, concerned about his popularity, deposed him in a *coup d'état* that triggered the political conflict in which the country is still embroiled. After the coup Thaksin was accused of corruption and fled to Dubai, where he remained until 22 August 2023, returning to Thailand as a result of a post-election deal between the party closest to him and the military that many of his supporters felt to be a betrayal. He was arrested but then released after a few months for medical reasons and thereafter accused of *lèse-majesté*. (C.S.)

a friend and fellow soldier accused of discharging his firearm while on leave.

The following year Anon started working in the field of human rights, defending activists protesting about environmental destruction in the northeast and south of Thailand. In 2010, after the military crackdown, he turned his attention to defending Red Shirt activists, taking on the first cases of what would become both his speciality and his alleged crime: *lèse-majesté*. After the 2014 *coup d'état* many *lèse-majesté* cases were moved to the military courts where Anon had cut his teeth, making him one of few lawyers in Thailand able and willing to defend those accused.

That was the year in which I met Anon for the first time, in the offices of Thai Lawyers for Human Rights, an organisation he had recently co-founded. As I entered his office on the second floor of a small residential building, Anon welcomed me from behind a huge desk covered in stacks of paper and half-finished plates of his favourite *larb*, a meat salad from the northeast. With a knowing smile and a joke about the ravenous look I had given the dishes, he promptly offered me some food before launching into a long, detailed explanation of the difficulties of defending clients against accusations of *lèse-majesté*.

'In many cases,' he told me, 'defendants spoke the truth, but many people in Thai society find that unacceptable, and so the court will find them guilty anyway. Nonetheless, my role is to represent them, especially as many lawyers refuse to do so out of fear it would ruin their reputation or even lead to them being accused of *lèse-majesté* themselves. They are probably right; it will be my turn sooner or later.'

This first interaction was characteristic of Anon: his sense of humour, his love of food, his unflagging dedication to upholding the rights of the most marginalised and his readiness to put himself in the front line of the struggles, even though it put him at risk. Who better than he, then, to dress up as Harry Potter, publicly name He-Who-Must-Not-Be-Named and kickstart one of the most tumultuous weeks in Thailand's history?

That day would become famous among protesters as marking a new phase of politics in which the monarchy would be publicly taken to task. As those who were there on the day love to recall, Anon's words 'opened a crack in the sky'. But, once pierced, the sky had to be opened up for good.

*

Legend has it that in 1917 Lenin, in exile in Switzerland, said that 'there are decades where nothing happens and there are weeks where decades happen'. Visionary though he was, he could hardly have imagined that one such week would start with a fidgety Thai lawyer dressed up as Harry Potter standing beside a scarecrow with the face of a character from a fantasy world created by a British author. And yet, that's what happened.

Within a week, by 10 August, the protest had grown. Ten thousand people, the highest number recorded at a demonstration since Prayut took power in 2014, gathered on the campus of one of the country's most prestigious universities, continuing along the path forged by Anon. This time it was mostly students on the stage. Among them was Rung, a young student who would raise the bar higher. Following Anon's lead, Rung read out, hesitantly at first but then with ever-growing confidence, ten demands for reforms to the monarchy. These would be rather commonplace in any other constitutional monarchy, but in Thailand they would irremediably change the national political debate.

The demands were simple and to the point: allow parliament to examine the actions of the king; revoke the *lèse-majesté* law and grant amnesty to all those accused; make a clear division between the king's personal assets from those under the government's control; reduce the amount of the national

THE WORLD'S STRANGEST CONSTITUTION

Thailand's 2017 constitution is one of the strangest pieces of legislation in the history of modern democracies. Written and promulgated by the military junta of Prayut Chan-o-cha, it attempts to consolidate a totalitarian regime within a constitutional charter that makes provisions for elections. Drafted by a council comprised exclusively of men in uniform, the constitution was ratified in a referendum in which opponents were forbidden from campaigning by a rule dictating that 'people who propagate information deemed distorted, violent, aggressive, inciting or threatening so that voters do not vote or vote in a particular way' would be punished by up to ten years in prison. The constitution is still in effect in Thailand and provides for a parliament composed of five hundred elected representatives and 250 senators, who are nominated by a panel of ten people appointed by the military junta. This means that a party or coalition opposed to the military stands a chance of electing a prime minister only if they achieve 75 per cent of the vote, while a party allied with the military only needs 25 per cent to form a government. The day before it was ratified, the palace made changes to the constitution that voters had approved, allowing the king to reside overseas without naming a regent and granting him the power to personally manage future constitutional crises. (C.S.)

budget allocated to the monarch; abolish unnecessary royal agencies and transfer control of the others to the appropriate institutions; cease all donations from all royal charitable funds and make them transparent; stop the king from interfering in politics; put an end to excessive glorification of the monarchy; investigate the deaths and disappearances of political exiles and critics of the monarchy; and, finally, prohibit the king from endorsing any future *coup d'état*.

It had only been a week since Anon's speech, yet the country seemed transformed. Problems that were obvious to everyone but that no one had dared to discuss publicly were finally being debated in the open, first in front of a few hundred people and then thousands, sparking an unprecedented national reckoning. Weeks when decades happen, as the Russian revolutionary said.

But there's a lot left unsaid in that Lenin quote. Those words, in fact, were not uttered at the height of his success but during one of his darkest moments, after a failed attempt had driven him and many of his comrades into exile. As Lenin was experiencing first-hand, decades condensed into such short periods of time do not simply vanish but roll back around, trying to make up for lost time, arresting the progress made in those weeks.

The counter-reformation, to use an old-fashioned term, was not long in coming, armed with the *lèse-majesté* law. Although such accusations had not been used since Vajiralongkorn's succession to the throne in 2016, they came back into fashion in August 2020. Since then at least 270 people have been charged – among them, unsurprisingly, are both Anon and Rung.

Charges against the two 'agitators'

were brought by Nopadol Prompasit, an extremely active member of the Thailand Help Centre for Cyberbullying Victims, one of many online groups of self-appointed defenders of the monarchy. Anon has since entered a spiral of trials, releases on bail and further charges, which landed him in jail in September 2023 and where he is still now detained awaiting fourteen further trials. These charges, used to suffocate political debate, are not limited to individuals such as Anon and Rung but have become, in the hands of the Constitutional Court and the electoral commission, tools to disband entire political parties.

On 14 May 2023 elections were held, and the Move Forward Party, the successor to the previously disbanded Future Forward Party, won by a landslide. Running on a platform centring the constitutional reforms demanded by the 2020 protests, they won 38 per cent of the vote, while Prayut's party fell to less than 13 per cent, losing half their parliamentary seats. The armed forces managed to stay in power despite this, thanks to a scandalous deal with Thaksin Shinawatra's former party, who betrayed their voters in exchange for amnesty for their founder. A few months later the Constitutional Court declared the Move Forward Party's proposal of reforms to Article 112 of the Criminal Code an act of *lèse-majesté* and an attempt to topple the constitutional monarchy, starting the process of dissolving the party and banning its executives from taking any public office for ten years.

This surge in *lèse-majesté* accusations, however, did not stop the protests, which simply changed form. From the end of 2020 the protests moved first to the police stations to which defendants were called to respond to charges and then to the courts every time there was a bail hearing. From there they have spread beyond Bangkok to provincial towns where small groups of protesters hold daily silent vigils lasting 112 minutes, once again adopting a new code to criticise the law.

*

Anon continues his mission as lawyer for the oppressed even while in prison, now wearing a different costume. He leaves jail almost every morning in a striped uniform and with shackles around his ankles to be escorted to courtrooms where, in spite of everything, he continues to represent other political prisoners. These long days in court, the only moments in which Anon gets to see his children, end with evenings back in his cell spent writing long letters to his family, which are almost immediately posted to his Facebook profile and read by thousands.

The letters, as heart-warming as they are devastating, are a testament to how political struggle is birthed and nurtured in everyday life, in the small, unremarkable actions that make us human. Anon's words offer a glimpse into the daily lives of political prisoners in Thailand, their solidarity and friendship in impossible situations, the sorrow of not being able to see your children grow up or embrace your loved ones and the pride of feeling, despite it all, that you're in the right – that you're struggling for a better world, greater democracy and a more tolerant society. In these letters Anon goes from making bombastic political declarations to expressing fear that his children, to whom the letters are mostly addressed, will slowly forget about him or be made fun of at school because their dad is in

Top: A demonstrator in Bangkok calls for democracy and demands justice for the Red Shirts who died in the 2010 military crackdown.
Bottom: The coffin of Netiporn Sanesangkhom, known as Bung, at her funeral in a Bangkok, May 2024. Bung was a political activist who called for reform of the monarchy and was jailed and charged under Article 112, the *lèse-majesté* law, and died while on hunger strike.

THE ANTI-CORRUPTION PIMP

Rather than a lawyer or a political activist, Thailand's most iconic anti-corruption hero of recent decades, Chuwit Kamolvisit, is a pretty colourful figure. In a previous life he was a pimp, the eccentric king of the capital's brothels who liked to have his photo taken in the Jacuzzi surrounded by some of the two thousand sex workers on his books. Officially, prostitution is banned in Thailand, but everyone knows what goes on in the massage parlours like the ones Chuwit operated. To gain licences for his erotic spas he had to bribe the police, which he did with great generosity until he went too far and lost his police protection. In January 2003 four hundred enforcers razed a Bangkok apartment building to the ground, ejecting the tenants; it soon emerged that the parcel of land had been bought some time before by our reckless businessman, who then found himself in the dock. After serving a month in jail Chuwit declared war on his former allies in uniform, reporting the officials he had been bribing for years and causing a scandal of unprecedented proportions. From there it was only a short step to a career in politics, a move that saw him stand twice for mayor and serve two terms in parliament. His popularity rose even higher when he became a TV presenter, however controversial. He has continued to denounce corruption in politics and the police even after being diagnosed with advanced liver cancer.

prison. His letters detail how to make the pork soup that his son Issarann, who was born in 2022, loves so much. They tenderly describe a little bird who comes to sit on his windowsill every morning and movingly convey how strange it is to continue defending clients while himself wearing a prison uniform.

'Being a lawyer in prison is wonderfully bizarre and in no way a problem at all. It's a little uncomfortable because I am shackled, but I can still work on my cases,' he writes. In other letters he reflects: 'The journey of a human rights lawyer becoming a political prisoner and the reversal of my fate made me understand the value of life and what the most important goals are' and 'My lawyer's gown is covered in dust and creased from the journey. It is wet with a mix of tears born of dashed hopes and tears born of fulfilled hopes. This gown does not serve the capitalists or the oppressors, it serves the villagers and the oppressed.'

In one letter, addressed to Pran, his eldest daughter, Anon writes: 'Daddy wants Pran to show Issarann a photograph of the 3 August 2020 speech and tell him, "Your father is Harry Potter, he is the lawyer Anon." Just the thought of that brings a satisfied smile to his dad's face as he is locked in his cell writing this letter, happy to see his children grow up in a better society.'

Anon is not the only one still convinced that change in Thai society is inevitable. Since the earliest arrests a joke has been circulating on Twitter, evidence of how humour remains one of the sharpest weapons in the arsenal of young Thais. 'Don't worry,' protesters encourage each other, 'Thai prisons aren't big enough for all of us.'

The king is dead, long live the king: A brief history of the Kingdom of Thailand

1932–3
The story of contemporary Thailand begins with a bloodless military coup, the 'Siamese Revolution of 1932'. The absolute monarchy is overthrown and the Kingdom of Siam becomes a constitutional monarchy. The coup is planned by a group of university students and young army officers, including the progressive Pridi Banomyong, the future 'father of Thai democracy', and the soldier and future dictator Plaek Phibunsongkhram (aka 'Phibun'), all of them members of the underground Khana Ratsadon party. But one coup leads to another (actually around twenty more take place up to 2014, twelve of them successful), and the following year the military faction of the movement takes over.

1935–40
After putting down a monarchist rebellion that ends in 1935 with the abdication of King Prajadhipok (Rama VII), who is succeeded by the nine-year-old Ananda Mahidol (Rama VIII), Phibun is named prime minister and installs a dictatorial regime inspired by fascism (even down to the salutes) in tandem with an ultra-nationalist Cultural Revolution aiming to integrate the Chinese, Shan and Lao minorities into a mono-ethnic nation through a process of forced Thaification. In 1939 the English name of the country is changed from Siam to Thailand.

1941–2
Thailand attacks French Indochina and gains territory in Laos and Cambodia. When the Japanese army lands in Thailand a few hours after the Pearl Harbor attack, Phibun agrees to grant the troops passage towards the British territories of Malaysia and Burma. He then declares war on the Allies and takes advantage of the Japanese advance to occupy the Burmese states of Shan and Kayah. A democratic opposition movement, Seri Thai, forms around Pridi Banomyong.

1944–6
Phibun is forced to resign when the tide turns in the war. With the Japanese defeat, Thailand also has to return its occupied territories. King Ananda returns from exile in 1945 but is discovered in his bed with a bullet in his head in an incident that has never been fully explained. He is succeeded by his brother Bhumibol Adulyadej, who reigns as Rama IX until his death in 2016. King Ananda's death weakens Pridi's elected civilian government, which alienates domestic conservative elites as well as the West with its strongly progressive policies, such as nationalisation and the assignment of land to cooperatives.

1947–57
Phibun returns to power following a coup, with the assistance of the USA, which appreciates his anti-communist stance. He governs behind a façade of democracy, allying himself with the West in the Korean War in exchange for major economic support and intensifying his policies aimed at reducing the influence of the Chinese diaspora. He survives various attempted coups and even takes a stab at democracy following a visit to the West in 1955, but he is ultimately

forced to give way to a new generation of military men supported by the USA.

1957–73
General Sarit Thanarat and, following his death in 1963, his second-in-command Thanom Kittikachorn establish a brutal military regime, co-opting the crown to provide them with legitimacy, restoring many of the powers it lost in 1932 and ushering in a long-term alliance between the army and the monarchy. Thailand offers its air bases to the Americans and sends troops to fight in Vietnam, while the governments in Hanoi and Beijing retaliate by funding a long and bloody communist guerrilla campaign in the north, northeast and south of the country. A demographic explosion accompanied by massive foreign investments, improvements in public education and large-scale urbanisation transform the economy and society.

1973–6
A student uprising, accompanied by large-scale anti-government demonstrations, causes the king to send Thanom into exile, ushering in a brief but significant period of freedom and democracy – as well as government instability. The fall of Saigon in 1975 terrifies the anti-communists, who are also unsettled by major strikes and an influx of refugees from Laos and Cambodia. On 6 October 1976, a few hours after the massacre of students and workers at Bangkok's Thammasat University at the hands of the police and far-right paramilitaries, a coup brings the military back to power.

1976–91
A series of military regimes are interspersed with coups. The communist guerrilla uprising dies out in 1983 following the promise of an amnesty, while Thai troops clash with the Vietnamese forces occupying Cambodia. The 1980s see a slow process of democratisation overseen by the king and General Prem Tinsulanonda, who reintroduces elections (an arrangement dubbed 'Premocracy'), accompanied by an economic boom; over the decade from 1985 Thailand grows faster than any other nation. In 1991 yet another military coup, this time successful, installs a civilian as prime minister, the competent reformer Anand Panyarachun.

1992–6
The army retakes power, but the population have had enough and organise huge demonstrations, which are bloodily put down in what becomes known as 'Black May'. The king intervenes on live television to act as a peacemaker between the two parties. Democracy is restored, and an elected assembly approves a new 'people's constitution' with explicit protections for human rights. Mired in scandals and corruption, Thailand's governments come and go.

1997–2000
A rapid devaluation of the baht triggers the Asian financial crisis, leading to bankruptcies and unemployment. The IMF intervenes. The economy soon bounces back, however, and in 2003 the country repays its debt ahead of schedule.

2001–4
The era of the businessman and populist politician Thaksin Shinawatra (aka 'the Asian Berlusconi') begins with an electoral triumph. He enjoys immense popularity in rural regions for his anti-poverty policies but is accused of authoritarianism and corruption by his opponents. He responds

with a crackdown on the increased violence in the Muslim-majority provinces of the south, leading to further violence. In 2004 a tsunami hits the country's western coasts, killing around eight thousand people and decimating the tourist industry.

2005–10
Thaksin is re-elected, but following protests by the monarchist, reactionary Yellow Shirt movement, the prime minister is overthrown in a (bloodless) coup while attending the UN General Assembly. The military junta is unable to contain Thaksin's influence, as his supporters, the Red Shirts, take to the streets several times in large-scale demonstrations in 2009, occupying part of central Bangkok for weeks in 2010. The army's clampdown claims at least ninety victims.

2011–14
The reincarnation of Thaksin's party wins the elections, and his sister Yingluck becomes prime minister. Severe floods cause hundreds of deaths and displace millions more. Attempts to obtain an amnesty for Thaksin lead to a new wave of protests between 2013 and 2014 that end with the removal of Yingluck. The World Bank upgrades Thailand to an upper-middle-income nation, and Bangkok becomes the world's most visited city for the first time.

2014–20
Under the leadership of General Prayut Chan-o-cha, the army declares martial law, takes power in a coup and begins harsh repression of opposition elements. Accusations of *lèse-majesté* come thick and fast. The king dies in 2016; after his seventy-year reign, he is seen as a figure of stability and moral authority and is succeeded by his son Vajiralongkorn (Rama X), who inspires the opposite feelings. In 2019 Prayut finally allows elections, out of which a new progressive party, Future Forward, emerges but is dissolved on constitutional grounds. In January 2020 the first case of Covid-19 outside China is recorded in Thailand.

2020–4
The pandemic damages an economy focused on tourism, particularly from China, but the sector recovers rapidly. Protests against the junta resume after the lockdowns, and the first voices openly critical of the monarchy are heard. The government uses force and the Covid-19 state of emergency to disperse and arrest the demonstrators. The 2023 elections are won by a coalition between the new incarnations of Thaksin's party and Future Forward, now known as Move Forward, but Thaksin aligns himself with the military and the monarchists, supporting a government led by Prime Minister Srettha Thavisin, who was succeeded the following year by Thaksin's daughter Paetongtarn Shinawatra. In 2024 parliament legalises gay marriage.

Becoming Bangkokian: How to Be a Hyphen-Thai

Thai identity and that of Bangkok are often conflated, even by the capital's inhabitants themselves. So what makes you a Bangkokian? And what distinguishes a Thai from a foreigner living in this metropolis in the heart of Asia?

PHILIP CORNWEL-SMITH

Tourists enjoying a meal at a seafood restaurant run by Thai-Chinese on Yaowarat Road in Bangkok's old Chinatown.

Wend your way through Ban Somdet Chao Phraya community (number ❹ on the map on page 36), and the Thai capital's ethnic variety pops out at every turn. In this block, hidden behind the Sikh shrine at Ban Khaek ❸, hamlets of Lao, Mon and Central Thai crafts folk live in knots of lanes beside Hokkien Chinese. Nearby Nurulmubeen Mosque and graveyard ❷ are tended by descendants of Malay silversmiths, brought here from Satun 150 years ago by a noble from the Bunnag clan of Persian ancestry. These peoples all live peacefully within one square kilometre, within a city born of migrants, within a land of seventy-two ethnicities – now all hyphenated 'Thai-'.

I am a hyphenated Englishman, resident for half my life in Bangkok. A writer by profession, I ended up documenting its street life, subcultures, arts and communities like Ban Somdet. Unlike the city's multifarious peoples, I'll never be a hyphen-Thai. I'm a forever foreigner, but as an émigré *flâneur*, having become an outsider-turned-insider in this most obliging of lands is a satisfying state of limbo.

I arrived in Thailand in 1994 as a listings journalist on my way back from Australia. Some expatriates come here to find a new identity. I merely wanted to experience its culture but found myself reinvented by Thailand, starting with three transformative experiences.

First, I studied Vipassana meditation on a ten-day silent retreat at Wat Suan Mokkh, founded in the South by the reformist monk Buddhadasa Bhikkhu. Its 4 a.m.–9 p.m. regimen reformatted habitual patterns to open a space for change – and I made breakthrough decisions in its wake. Not allowed to speak, I felt other senses intensify. I'm not Buddhist, but the insights opened my senses and aligned my mind to Thailand.

I then learned traditional Northern Thai massage at ITM in Chiang Mai. As with meditation, this everyday Thai skill reinforces sensory perception: touch, posture, breathing, intuition, temperature, pain, herbal scent. These two courses taught me that the Thai mental furniture is not mysterious exotica but knowable. By the time I reached Bangkok after seven weeks upcountry, I was beginning to 'read' Thai culture.

My third transformation was being offered a job unimaginable in my jaded homeland. Thailand was in its Asian Tiger Cub boom, bubbling with opportunities. Within four days of visiting Bangkok I was hired to set up its first city magazine, *Bangkok Metro*. Ever

---

PHILIP CORNWEL-SMITH is a British writer, photographer and curator who lives between Thailand and Bali. His influential bestseller *Very Thai: Everyday Popular Culture*, first published in 2004, has become a go-to text and style reference that defines the category of informal urban Thainess. The follow-up, *Very Bangkok: In the City of the Senses* (2020), explains his adopted city from multiple fresh perspectives and is now out in an updated second edition.

> 'For centuries multiple peoples have settled – sometimes have been forcibly resettled – in this crossroads country.'

since, Bangkok has been my home and my subject.

*

Polyglot Bangkok is a city of settlers that willingly hosts people of any origin. Thais have a 400-year history of hiring foreign expertise. Today my adoptive city has one of the biggest and most varied expatriate populations in the world.

The capital sprawls into six other provinces, but within the Bangkok Metropolitan Administration, out of 6.9 million residents in the 2010 census, half were Chinese-Thai. The rest were 3.14 million kinds of ethnic Thais, 207,000 Indian-Thais, 140,000 Westerners, 70,000 Japanese, 35,000 Arabs, 35,000 Africans and 70,000 other East Asians, who would have since been swelled by a massive Chinese influx. Uncountable numbers come and go from the provinces, with many foreign migrants being undocumented, so no one knows precisely how many live here.

For centuries multiple peoples have settled – sometimes have been forcibly resettled – in this crossroads country. Its scores of ethnic villages are living museums that draw tourist and local curiosity. As intermarriage continues and young residents move out, those cultural distinctions dissolve into the mainstream. In this era of migration crises, Thailand's peaceful absorption of minorities is a rare success. Bangkok has avoided most of the racial chauvinism and communal violence that's plagued several ASEAN neighbours. Bangkok's Muslims live calmly among other beliefs, despite a Malay insurgency in Thailand's Deep South. Ever since Chinese gangs were pacified a century ago, huge effort has gone into building social harmony.

'Unlike the West, where race and ethnicity can often result in riots and lynching, and all sorts of discrimination, this isn't really an issue,' writes columnist Voranai Vanijaka in the *Bangkok Post*. 'There's no Lao Pride Parade. No Malay Affirmative Action Group. The trouble in the Deep South is political, where ethnicity and religion are used as tools. But other than that, the central authority has done a great job through the years, of melting everyone into the Thai identity. The difference is in social class, divided by wealth, rather than ethnicity.'

Southeast Asia has extremely varied DNA, creeds and languages, yet Thailand has long been touted as somehow homogenous, mostly due to the nation-building ideology called 'Thainess'. The *CIA World Factbook* ranks it the eighth-most monoethnic country at 97 per cent Thai, but it's more complex than that. The region has sixty-two kinds of Tai tribes, twenty-four of them in Thailand. Other counts put Thais at 77 per cent with many subgroups. Around four in ten citizens are kinds of Lao, yet since 1905 censuses have excluded a 'Lao' category, so Thai-Lao can only pick 'Thai'. Crucially, two-fifths of Bangkokians have at least some Chinese genes. In the journal *Sinlapa Watthanatham* historian Sujit Wongthes described the result as 'Jek bon Lao' (Chinese upon Lao), while

in an interview with me, Northern Thai expert Vithi Phanichphant, himself part Chinese, described Bangkokians as the 'Hinduised Chinese'.

*

Assimilation has gone in phases: natural, then forced and now with secondary identities tolerated. Old Siam had been like the Austro-Hungarian Empire: a pan-ethnic, shape-shifting territory under a 'Universal King' who accrued prestige the more minorities he ruled. Bangkok was its Vienna – the cosmopolitan imperial seat.

During the nation-building era, forced assimilation fused a singular nationality. Bangkok, as the immigrant gateway, was the crucible for this melting pot. Compulsory Thainess bonded the regions and acculturated the influx from China, India and beyond. Cultural differentiation was banned – even noting Thais as being Southern or Northern – under the blanket phrase still used constantly: 'All Thais'.

Reflecting the global multicultural trend, assimilation is now more negotiable. Internal migrants brought their local values, and minorities began calling for recognition. Once ethnicity felt less of a threat, their heritage came to be treated as historical curios. Many now hyphenate Thai- with their race, like Thai-Indian, and some feel multiple sub-identities. Bangkok is like a stir-fry, a Thai cooking style of Chinese origin that leaves each ingredient distinct.

The term 'Thai' is a paradox: it is both a description of what is and a prescription of what should be. When outsiders see the messy reality and reach for an adjective, they assume 'Thai' includes the informal popular culture, when that's almost the opposite. The national identity, Thai, is taken as an imperative to overcome those undisciplined traits and perform the gracious cultural ideal, in line with social pressure and instructions by the state. Thainess is part delight, part duty. It is best understood as a social contract of nation-building that has changed over time, even reversing stances on Sino-Thais and modernity. Its well-documented history includes King Rama V (reigned 1868–1910) coining the civilising concept of *siwilai*, King Rama VI (reigned 1910–25) promoting nationalism and his brother Prince Damrong Rajanubhab being dubbed the 'Father of Thai History' because he codified Thai national heritage.

In the 1930s and 40s the dictator Field Marshal Phibunsongkhram distilled Thainess into a 'national culture' under the martial influence of German *Kultur*, Italian fascism and Japanese bushido. His Twelve Cultural Mandates changed the country's name and continue to steer policy to this day. The ideologue Luang Vichit-Vadhakan instilled the performance of Thainess through new 'traditional' dances, moralistic plays and the patriotic songs still broadcast in public spaces at festival times.

Royalist nationalism, galvanised since 1957 under military dictators, a revival of

Opposite from top: Commuters on Bangkok's BTS Skytrain; a view of the Chao Phraya River, which flows through Bangkok, from the roof of the King Power Mahanakorn skyscraper, a modern luxury hotel and residential block; young celebrities dress up as students and jam with rock bands in a public square at Centerpoint Siam Square in central Bangkok, a meeting place for many young people.

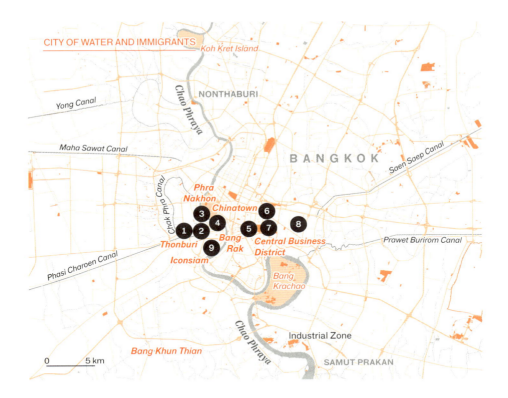

noblesse oblige and devotion to King Bhumibol's seventy-year reign (1946–2016) for his embodiment of traditional virtues. In the 1980s General Prem Tinsulanonda's premiership instituted a National Culture Commission, spectacular pageantry and the National Identity Board, which after the 1997 crash decreed five Thai virtues to obey and twelve un-Thai values to avoid. Similar strictures followed the 2014 coup, with children tested on memorising the junta's Twelve Core Values. This penchant for numbered lists echoes Buddhism's itemised ethics such as the Four Noble Truths and the Eightfold Path.

*

'Strangely enough, the self-proclaimed heralds of whatever constitutes "Thai- ness" are all from Bangkok, dictating to the rest of the country what "Thainess" is supposed to be,' journalist Saksith Saiyasombut said to me. This poses a conundrum. Official Thainess distils an essence of Bangkokness, yet Bangkok clearly violates tenets of Thainess.

When writing my book *Very Bangkok*, I sought to differentiate Bangkokness from Thainess. Yet whenever I asked residents about Bangkok's distinctiveness, most repeated the generic script of Thainess plus criticisms of its flawed urbanism. The city's identity is cramped by how strongly Bangkokians identify with Nation, showing a fervour akin to *Juche* in North Korea.

'Bangkok culture is not represented in the official culture,' documentary filmmaker Ing K told me. 'Meanwhile, organic Thai culture, including the urban and especially the intellectual, is discouraged.' While Bangkok contains migrants and traits from all over the country, it radically differs from the provinces, even the surrounding Central Plains. Bangkok is a bona fide megalopolis with 'world city' kudos in a country that became majority-urban in 2012, around the same time as the planet. While its citizens seem proud of the capital's national role, they're ambivalent about its own city-ness.

'Thais aren't like Westerners where they have New York pride or Liverpool pride. We don't have that strong city-based identity,' Voranai put to me. 'There's no rivalry. It is understood that Bangkok is the centre of the Thai universe.' Thai beliefs take that statement literally. The Old Town was laid out as a *mandala* – a physical and mental map of Hindu/Buddhist cosmology under the *chakravatin*, the Universal King. Today's capital inherits that mindset. Those closer to power gain more status, lending Bangkokians an aura over the Thai world.

The slogan 'City of Angels' conjures Orientalist allure, but it wasn't invented for tourism. It's the literal translation of Krung Thep, the start of the city's formal title, which *Guinness World Records* lists, at sixty-four syllables, as the world's longest place name. It reads like a résumé of sacred credentials, translating as 'Great city of angels, the supreme repository of the divine jewels, the supreme unconquerable land of the immortal divinity (Indra) endowed with the nine noble gems, the delightful capital city abounding in royal palaces, which resemble heavenly paradises for the reincarnated deities, commissioned by Indra for Vishnukam to create'. In this sense, Thais revere Krung Thep as one gigantic offering.

Unlike other mandalic cities – which are either ruins like Angkor or desacralised like Mandalay or Beijing's Forbidden City – Bangkok remains active as a sacred site. The king, high officials and Brahmin priests perform that cosmology through rituals like the Royal Ploughing Ceremony.

Capitals inherently act superior, but Bangkok indulges in self-praise: City of Angels, non-colonised dynastic realm, lead city of Buddhism. It is rivalled as a regional hub only by Singapore, and since 2012 has most years been the world's most visited city.

The fantastical imagery in Thainess festivals or the Songkran – Thai New Year – parade prompts cognitive dissonance, given the looming skyscrapers and elevated trains. This 'auto-orientalist' mythology is partly for tourism but also for domestic reinforcement. Since the mid-19th century Bangkok has sought to embody two contrary legitimacies: an ancient history – centred on court, pastoral tradition and a divine mantle – while also claiming that it's up to date.

Beyond Thai exceptionalism from the rest of the world, Bangkokians often assert their exceptionalism within Thailand, whether in education, taste, success, discipline or political judgement. Bangkok-centricity is not just in the Thai mind but hardwired into the infrastructure as the world's most primate city, dominating its hinterland to a greater extent than any other country's leading city. The country revolves around what the capital wants. Yet there's little celebration of Bangkok as its own phenomenon. Its modernity is viewed as state development, its skyscrapers as *siwilai* and city people as generic Thais. There's no coherent framing of its commerce, street life or handmade transit vehicles as forms of culture.

The dominant kind of Bangkok building is the shophouse – a Chinese format of row or terrace houses where people live above open-fronted work spaces – but this mass phenomenon has only recently been recognised as a cultural motif and preserved as heritage only in cases where they were built by nobles.

*

I observed this disjoint with curiosity. Cities and popular culture are a focus of my writing, so it was a boon to encounter such unexplored possibilities. I'd learned consumer journalism in Britain at Time Out Publications, where I was deputy editor of the first *Time Out London City Guide*, which reinvented guidebooks by focusing more on engaging with the local way of life than with sights. After eight years editing *Bangkok Metro* magazine I rejoined Time Out to edit its first *Bangkok City Guide*. Youth and community subcultures had been largely absent from coverage of Thainess or tourism promotion. Half of *Time Out Bangkok*'s listings had never been in a guidebook, although those scenes have since become staples in guides, tours and promotion.

As an editor, I was asked a lot of questions. I was familiar with Thai entertainment, lifestyle and where to go for food or music but flummoxed by queries such as why do schoolgirls wear sailor suits and Chulalongkorn University footballers play in pink? Decoding such puzzles became my next mission in writing the book *Very Thai: Everyday Popular Culture*. Informal street life was (and often still is) treated as 'low' and not 'Thai', but by legitimising such taboo topics as culture, *Very Thai* became the go-to source book for young creatives, who started exploring everyday urban themes in art and design, events and advertising. The book took on a life of its own, being curated by others as an exhibit in at least six exhibitions. 'Very Thai' even became a term for informal culture, to differentiate it from formal Thainess. As one Thai artist put it, '*Very Thai* coined the category.'

Similar gaps plague the understanding of Bangkok. Books and articles on the city tended to focus on a select few downtown landmarks, with either academic or promotional aims, but missing its deeper character. So in *Very Bangkok* I sought to portray the metropolis from multiple perspectives, delving into its communities, subcultures and distinctive structure. Bangkok appears chaotic, but beneath the messy surface it's an ambiguous, adaptive urban organism that's startlingly well organised. Its order is not visual but social.

To overcome Bangkok's stubborn reputations – exotic, smiling, sleazy, genteel, corrupt, shallow – I also interpreted the city through twenty senses. We all have more than the basic five senses, and those perceptions can reveal traits particular to each culture. Our conditioned responses miss things that our bodily senses can notice through experience in the moment, which is more in tune with Thai ways of thinking.

*

The Western model of what a city should be makes Asian megalopolises seem distorted by-products of modernity and globalisation, whereas they are cultural responses to local issues, whether dense living or as an embodiment of ideologies or beliefs. 'The city in the non-West is often disregarded as a phenomenon in its own right, with its own distinctive

'The Western model of what a city should be makes Asian megalopolises seem distorted by-products of modernity and globalisation, whereas they are cultural responses to local issues.'

history, traditions, rhythms, meanings and senses of place,' writes Annette Hamilton in *Wonderful, Terrible: Everyday Life in Bangkok*. Its messy ingenuity is precisely why sci-fi writers style Bangkok as a possible model for handling an untidy apocalyptic future.

'Traditional popular urbanism was never proclaimed – it just was,' says sociologist Marc Askew in his book *Bangkok: Place, Practice and Representation*. From the earlier Siamese capital of Ayutthaya (destroyed in 1767), Bangkok inherited two characteristics: being atomised and amphibious. Both were 'water cities', an East Asian urban form often dubbed 'Venice of the East', except that, unlike Venice, most residents lived not on drained land but over the water in stilt houses, boats or bamboo raft huts, linked along the waterways to create floating precincts dubbed 'riverside ribbon urbanism'.

To explain the city-ness of Bangkok also requires acknowledging the role of non-Thais in its making. Minorities were controlled by confining them to self-managed enclaves. Bangkok remains a patchwork of 'urban hamlets' fed by dead-end *sois* rather than an interconnected lattice. Unlike the ghettos within foreign cities, the entire conurbation was compartmentalised.

'Bangkok was not perceived as a distinct urban phenomenon but as a type of extreme densification of rural habitation,' explains the aristocratic architect Chittawadi Chitrabongs in *The Politics of Defecation in Bangkok of the Fifth Reign*. Housing, production and trade kept a village quality. Temples were the focus of health, schooling and entertainments. 'While [the Victorian-era king] Rama V was enthusiastic about importing objects of modernity, he did not introduce an alternative way of life to Bangkok's inhabitants.'

Communities could maintain their social structure because enclaves weren't well interlinked, while their allotted specialist trades gave them a particular role in city life. Nationalist regimes sought to break their local organisation and switch the citizen's fealty to country. Thainess does not equate to tradition, and the various regional traditions are being relentlessly subsumed into Bangkok's uniform Thainess. Identifying as a metropolitan Thai is very recent and is most expressed by young creatives who grew up under the 1988–2014 era of partial democracy.

Under the prevailing development-state mentality, Bangkok's dense rural habitation was deemed backward. Canals were filled in, floating houses banned and wooden homes cleared for concrete construction. From the mid-1960s Bangkok exploded as a hybrid metropolis in a largely free-market experiment, with poorly planned development and disconnected transport systems. It's been the Thai gateway to what's new in the world. The result is

Visitors to the Grand Palace in Bangkok passing the Chakri Maha Prasat throne hall.

THE VERTICAL CITY

In 2001, after nearly twenty years of economic boom and urbanisation – only briefly interrupted by the 1997 crisis – half of Thailand's urban population were living in Bangkok. Since then the city has not stopped growing. The expansion has been horizontal, in what is termed ribbon development – along the newly built roads and the route of the BTS Skytrain elevated mass rapid transit system – as well as vertical: the city has well over a hundred skyscrapers standing more than 150 metres tall, putting it thirteenth among the world's 'tallest' cities. At 318 metres, the most imposing (at least for now) is the Magnolia Waterfront Residences tower, part of the vast riverside Iconsiam complex ❾, which is also home to the country's second-largest shopping centre. A city plan was approved in 2013, but the rapid pace of development has made it difficult to apply, and the city is facing major environmental and social problems – traffic, first and foremost, with the resulting air pollution, the lack of green spaces and the persistent presence of informal settlements with limited access to public services. On top of this, and underlining the extreme inequality that characterises the country, gentrification is advancing, a phenomenon captured in Prempapat Plittapolkranpim's documentary *The Last Breath of Sam Yan* (2023), which tells of the fight to preserve a shrine at risk of demolition to make way for the expansion of Bangkok's leading university.

a city ensnared by corporations, towers and suburban sprawl – ways of living that divorced Bangkok both from its own roots and from the provinces. Dominance by Bangkok became a core issue in Thailand's social and political tensions. The heavily urban Yellow Shirts mocked the largely rural origins of the Red Shirts, whose occupation of central shopping districts in 2010 was meant and felt as an affront to the downtown elite (see 'Yellows and Reds' on page 14). When that encampment was violently cleared, a spree of arson and an emotive clean-up by volunteers spurred the emergence of a pride in Bangkok among the affluent classes. The same incident made poorer residents question if the city really belonged to them.

'Many Bangkokians still think that there is some underdeveloped wild savage hinterland beyond the city borders and look with weariness and condescension to the rest of the country,' Saksith adds. 'There really is a belief that this city has its own set of rules and laws. A saying has it that Thailand has never been colonised by anybody, except by Bangkok. Look at that satirical Facebook page "Prathet Krung Thep" – "Country of Bangkok".'

*

Settlers have a different stake in Bangkok than those born in the city. First or even second generations treat the capital in practical, transactional terms, as a necessary step to advancement. Wistfully they regard 'home' as their provincial origin, to which they send remittances and return on holidays. Lately, though, some rural migrants now skip to the growing provincial cities that have broken Bangkok's former monopoly on Thai urbanism.

Migrant histories had been smothered by the national narrative. Their roots get glossed over as 'ethnic colour', omitting painful specifics. Settlers and war captives didn't want to dwell on why they came, so they suppressed their ancestry and built fresh futures as Thai. That tension remains palpable in attention to accent, manners and skin tone.

Both Thais and foreigners tend to paint Thai nationalism as a defence against the Western colonial encroachment that defined the borders, but its internal imperative was to absorb millions of Chinese migrants. Many authors of Thai nationalism had some Chinese ancestry and so knew from the heart what terms might work. 'Fourth-generation Chinese were unheard of,' according to a truism by anthropologist William Skinner, 'because all great-grandchildren of Chinese immigrants had merged with Thai society.'

The 1969 novel *Letters from Thailand* by Botan shocked Thais with its frank portrayal of this process. When a Chinese settler resists assimilation, his Bangkok-born daughter tells him (in Susan Fulop Kepner's translation): 'It's not something you decide to do. It happens in the normal course of things.' Later in the book her father concedes: 'I could not shelter them from the thousands of experiences which made them another people, another race. There are so many of us here, yet the Thai have won – the Chinese have turned into Thai.'

Assimilation isn't one directional, though; the host culture also changes. While Thai traditions survive more in rural areas, most Chinese settled in cities, where majorities tend to have paler Sinified features quite distinct from indigenous Thais.

Plenty of Chinese migrants were affluent, but the stereotype holds that most arrived poor, as the saying goes 'with just a mat and a pot', then pulled themselves up to the heights of society. 'Psychologically, most of the Chinese in Thailand see their ancestors as coming from peasant stock,' *The Encyclopaedia of the Chinese Overseas* quotes a young Sino-Thai professional, 'so believing in a culture is an upgrading for them.'

Sino-Thais often express gratitude for the chance to flourish more easily here than in China. The founder of the royalist Yellow Shirt movement, Hainan-born media mogul Sondhi Limthongkul, coined the term 'Sino-Thai patriot'. In speeches he recalled his mother's refusal to revisit China: 'Living 50 years under royal aegis, loving Thailand more than some native Thais, she said that Thailand was her home and she did not want ever to leave.'

Overall, due to physical and religious similarities, the Chinese and other Buddhists such as the Mon and Lao have integrated more smoothly than have the Hindus, Muslims, Christians or secular Westerners. While ethnic enclaves seem like benign attractions today, their diversity had been distrusted as a barrier

'Plenty of Chinese migrants were affluent, but the stereotype holds that most arrived poor, as the saying goes "with just a mat and a pot", then pulled themselves up.'

Tourists taking a tuk-tuk ride through Yaowarat, Bangkok.

to unity. The government redrew the boundaries of enclaves like Ban Somdet and replaced their local leadership with bureaucrats to instil allegiance to the state.

For decades some minorities advocated for recognition, eventually buoyed by a global trend to champion the Indigenous. Often it was youth who rekindled interest in the roots that their parents and grandparents had stifled. By the 2000s ethnicity wasn't seen as a threat and the national narrative began to accept minority heritage as long as it professed loyalty to Thainess. Now the multi-racial enclave of Kudi Jeen ❶ – with its legacies of Portuguese, Chinese, Mon and Shi'a Muslim – is being conserved as a project for Bangkok's 250th anniversary. Later arrivals have established colourful quarters, in tune with the city's aggregate style. Gulf families buy myrrh and puff on shisha pipes in Nana's Soi Arab ❽. Chaebol managers from Seoul eat bibimbap in Sukhumvit Plaza's Korea Town ❼, opposite the Manhattan Hotel where the first Korean visitors stayed. Japanese croon karaoke in the mini-Ginzas of Thaniya ❺ and around Thonglor's J-Avenue ❻.

Migration never stops, but Thailand isn't always a safe harbour. Immigration rules for 'aliens' keep shifting. Refugees and émigrés often get sent back, and the millions of migrant workers suffer discrimination and struggle to get the right papers. Expatriates face arcane hurdles around visas, residency and work permits, while the ninety-day reporting rule treats legal foreign residents as if they're on parole. Ever wary of takeover, never-colonised Thailand keeps non-Thais off-balance.

Expatriates are often equated with affluent Westerners, but here they're

Becoming Bangkokian: How to Be a Hyphen-Thai

Above: Cooling down during the Thai New Year celebrations.
Below: Young Bangkokians at the Corner House, a retro community space and historical relic in Talat Noi.

ITALO-THAI

Unbeknown to most people, much of the institutional architecture in Thailand is the work of Italians. Since the reign of King Rama IV (reigned 1851–68), under pressure on three sides from French expansion in Indochina and British activity in Malaya and Burma, Thailand found itself having to ward off the two European nations' expansionist aspirations. Given their military inferiority, the Thai kings defended themselves with international agreements aimed at putting the two powers at odds with each other and with the construction of a 'civilised' image of the country – in other words, more like Europe. As a result, slavery and polygamy were prohibited and, unlike neighbouring countries, the people of Thailand began to eat with forks and spoons, which is still the case to this day. Building institutional structures similar to their European counterparts became fundamental for the international image of the Thai kings – and what better source than the recently founded Kingdom of Italy's school of architecture and engineering. Between 1868 and the period following the Second World War, a string of Italian architects, engineers, painters and sculptors moved to Thailand and created some of Bangkok's most iconic buildings and monuments, including the Democracy Monument, the central railway station, the Victory Monument, the first headquarters of the Siam Commercial Bank, the throne room at Dusit Palace and the current prime minister's residence. To this day a reminder of this collaboration is to be found in the name of the country's largest construction firm, the Italthai Group, even though it is now 100 per cent Thai owned. (C.S.)

majority Asian – and always were. Across Southeast Asia, hiring Chinese and other foreign expertise was a centuries-old strategy to avoid empowering native subjects of the feudal rulers. A similar imbalance still restricts access to capital, power and the professions, a grievance that animates political movements against the establishment. Old Siam even had a Greek prime minister, a Japanese general, Dutch cannon-makers, a Dane to found the army, a Briton to lay the first sealed road and Italians to build palaces and ministries. Descendants of a Persian sheikh dominated Siamese officialdom from roughly 1600 to 1900. One who converted to Buddhism in the 1760s, Bunnag, founded a powerful lineage that still produces leaders.

This ambivalent city continues to feel at ease with an impermanent, floating population of unassimilated people. Aside from bureaucratic hurdles, they're mostly left free to be themselves. As well as diaspora settlers and expatriates, sojourners have been a 'Bangkok type' for centuries, working long enough to return home with savings – or reinventing themselves and staying put. Buddhist tolerance enables other ways of being, so it's a haven for social misfits, from bohemian artists and digital nomads to the gay diaspora. Western 'Easties', who feel that Asia is their spiritual home, often treat Bangkok as their favoured metropolis. Many of the unassimilated stay for decades, often for life.

In weighing Bangkok's character I've come to ponder how Bangkok has changed me and how I sense the world. Identity is often treated as definitive, but it's never pure or easily siloed, as shown by Bangkok's ethnic stir-fry. Like other unassimilated aliens, I can never feel Thai, but I can become Bangkokian.

Higher Powers

PITCHAYA SUDBANTHAD

A land of countless religious beliefs, for centuries Thailand has seen Buddhism intertwined with the power of the state. But, however hard the powers that be try to tame and centralise the religion, the authorities struggle to control the everyday practices of millions of people and traditions that depart from the 'official' school.

Monks at Wat Phra Dhammakaya, Bangkok, gather for meditation on Vesak, the day on which Buddhists celebrate the Buddha's birth, enlightenment and nirvana.

The rebel monk and my paternal grandparents sat staring at me. A family member who had found the image on the internet posted it to a message group where my elderly aunts and uncles liked to reminisce about times long past. The black-and-white photo was scanned from an unidentified newspaper, probably one of the defunct ones from the heyday of newsprint when newsboys criss-crossed Bangkok intersections and offered the latest edition for less than a baht. There's a good chance it was from the front page, because headlines about the rebel monk would have sold many copies, not only in the capital but everywhere in the country, especially in the Northern provinces. The rebel monk was facing serious allegations of mass incitement and had been ordered to stay sequestered at Wat Bawonniwet, a traditional temple of patronage for the country's ruling class.

In the photo, Khruba Siwichai sat between my grandparents and several young students who attended the school they were both running in the Nang Loeng area of Bangkok. My grandfather opened the school after his return from military duty in the Shan States, occupied by Thailand during the Second World War, along with the nurse from Lamphun province whom he'd met and married. My grandmother was descended from people who called themselves Yong after their home city in what is now Myanmar – as was Khruba Siwichai. She'd long admired him as a spiritual and leadership figure, so when he was sequestered in Bangkok she often brought him food and any simple item he needed for monastic comforts while a captive of the Sangha Supreme Council, the governing body of Thai Buddhism. My Uncle Jumpol told me this and added that he, too, was present in that photo taken at my grandparents' school but still inside his mother's womb. He missed his chance to also be able to stare back at me from a photo taken when Khruba Siwichai answered my grandmother's request to visit them after he had been summoned from the north of the country, where all the trouble with the Council – and the government – had started.

Buddhism plays its sizeable role as the dominant religion in the country, with more than 90 per cent of people identifying as Buddhist, far exceeding any other government-recognised faiths. As the official religion in Thailand, with its important ceremonial days counted as public holidays, Buddhism has been intertwined with the state since the 13th century when the first Thai kingdom of Sukhothai supported its spread from the south of Thailand by way of Sinhalese

PITCHAYA SUDBANTHAD is the author of *Bangkok Wakes to Rain* (2019). The novel was selected as a notable book of the year by *The New York Times* and *The Washington Post* as well as finalist for the Center for Fiction's First Novel Prize, the Chautauqua Prize, the Casa delle Letterature Bridge Book Prize and the Edward Stanford Award.

Top: A man pays respect to the Buddha on Vesak.
Bottom: A monk and a novice from Wat Phu Samanaram walk on Su Tong Pae, the bamboo bridge of faith and success, in Mae Hong Son, a province in Northern Thailand that borders Myanmar.

Higher Powers

THE PASSENGER   Pitchaya Sudbanthad

THE SPIRIT CAVE

As rescuers raced against time and extraordinary logistical difficulties to extract the young footballers trapped for more than two weeks in Tham Luang cave in the north of Thailand – in what became a major media spectacle followed with bated breath all around the world in the summer of 2018 – an entirely different story was playing out in Thailand on a symbolic level. According to a local belief the cave is home to the spirit of a princess of the old kingdom of Chiang Rung. After falling pregnant to a commoner she took refuge in the cave, where she later committed suicide, giving rise to the Mae Nam Mae Sai River (her blood) and the Doi Nang Non mountains (her reclining body, which gives the cave its nickname). It is very common in Thailand for caves to be regarded as magical places in which to make offerings to placate the spirits. In an article published by the online magazine *New Mandala*, Edoardo Siani, an expert on Thai Buddhism, interprets the transformation of the army's rescue operations into a media event as an assertion of centralised power over the 'wild' local spirit, which was dismissed as a mere superstition, while being overlaid with many images relating to Buddhist symbolism. From this perspective the narrative of the rescue put out by the authorities would represent yet another chapter in the centuries-old process of centralisation within Thailand and its religious sphere, in which the powers that be decide what is deemed superstition and what instead constitutes a noble Buddhist doctrine.

monks from Sri Lanka. This branch of Buddhism, commonly called the Theravada school, claims authoritative fidelity to Siddhartha Gautama's original teachings, and to this day Pali words said to have been uttered by the Buddha himself are still invoked in both everyday prayers and officiated ceremonies.

State patronage of Buddhism continued into the Ayutthaya era, by which time monks had attained eminent status in society. The Chevalier de Chaumont, the ambassador of King Louis XIV of France, wrote in a 1685 account of his embassy to the kingdom of Siam, as translated by Michael Smithies: 'The Talapoins are much reverenced by all the people and even the king himself; they cast not themselves on the ground when they speak to him, as the greatest in the kingdom do …' That partnership between religion and state would continue into the Rattanakosin period, as the island that would become Bangkok grew into a centre of power that would exert much influence on its far-flung territories and vassal domains, southwards into the Malay Peninsula and northwards into remnants of the Lanna kingdom and the ethnic Laotian areas, each already with its own localised variations of Buddhism and folk beliefs.

Opposite top: Statues of the four novices at the Chern Tawan International Meditation Centre in Northern Thailand embody Dharma philosophy: cover your ears and listen closely; cover your eyes to observe profoundly; cover your mouth and think before you speak; have an open heart and continue learning.
Opposite bottom: The monks organising a Vesak event at Wat Phra Dhammakaya.

A diversity of unorthodox views and practices did not sit well with the seat of power. Beginning in the 1820s Prince Mongkut, a monk who would become king, initiated reforms of Buddhist study and helped to found the Dhammayut order, meant to return Thai Buddhism to the fundamental written standards of the Pali Canon. This was how Thai Buddhism diverged into two orders: those in the minority but traditionally state-aligned Dhammayut order and the Mahanikaya order, which consists of all others, making up over 94 per cent of all temples.

A generation later more centralisation would arrive with the Sangha Act of 1902, steered by Prince Wachirayan, as an attempt to organise the country's Buddhism and its clergy into a more managed, scientific system influenced by Western modernisation and standardisation. There would be renewed emphasis on the canonical text, with routine examinations for monks' advancement up the ladder. To a ruling class, codes of ideal conduct, or *vinaya*, for both laypeople and monks, gained useful priority over the intangibles of the spiritual. The aspiration of enlightenment to nirvana would fall by the wayside, and its mention was even removed from the candidate statement in an ordination ceremony.

With subsequent amendments to the act, laws formulated in Bangkok would override any local traditions for the *sangha*, and abbots would see their autonomy erode, with deference to the Sangha Supreme Council and other regional figures appointed by way of the capital. Wandering monks who roamed through forests and temples, gaining the worshipful bows of villagers and claiming higher states of enlightenment,

ECO-BUDDHISM

The forest served as a refuge into which the Buddha withdrew for the purposes of his spiritual quest, and, in line with his teachings, the Theravada school of Buddhism regards forests as sacred. From the late 1980s, faced with the dramatic threat of deforestation, especially in Northern Thailand, a number of 'forest monks' abandoned their ascetic detachment from the world to lobby in defence of the land. Initially these forms of environmental activism – for example, protesting about dam-building projects – were risky undertakings: one monk was arrested for opposing the establishment of a eucalyptus plantation, while others were targeted with acts of intimidation. In 1988 the first ritual was performed to consecrate a tree, which was wrapped in the orange robes of a monk, a practice that has since become very common. Over time these spectacular acts have lost their radicalism, and the monks' environmentalism, which the researcher Amalia Rossi describes as 'eco-Buddhism' in an anthropological study, has become ever more aligned with the interests of the state, which in recent decades has turned towards environmental preservation, banning logging in 1989, creating nature reserves and parks and promoting an idea of wild nature. It is not uncommon for reforestation projects, supported by the city-dwellers, to clash with the interests of rural people. Often members of ethnic minorities, those living in these areas are excluded from the management of forest resources and see their traditional agricultural practices stigmatised.

> 'Also disturbing to the authorities were rumours of miraculous occurrences swirling around the monk: that he would not get wet in the rain or could walk on water.'

would need to comply or risk illegitimacy, but an official religious bureaucracy did not find favour with monks far from the seat of power – including the rebel monk whom my grandparents supported.

When Khruba Siwichai was called to the capital, it wasn't the first time he had faced the ire of the Council and regional authorities. In the 1910s he was detained several times for ordination ceremonies that purportedly did not comply with centralised rules, at a time when the Siamese kingdom was trying to assert and expand administrative control through both secular and religious laws in the absorbed northern Lanna kingdom, or Monthon Phayab as it had been renamed. Then in 1920 he had to defend himself in Lamphun and Bangkok against several charges, ranging from unlawful ordination to disobeying official orders. His popularity only surged. In the north thousands accompanied him, banging pots and blowing horns, as he reported to the temples where he would be detained.

When he appeared at my grandparents' school it was about fifteen years later, and he was yet again facing charges. This time they were for organising and completing a project to build a path up to Wat Phrathat Doi Suthep, a revered mountain-top temple in Chiang Mai, without official consent. This action coincided with monks from more than ninety temples in the north refusing to accept the authority of the Sangha Supreme Council and Karen tribespeople burning school furniture to protest at having to learn the Thai language as required by the government in an effort to create a unified national culture. Also disturbing to the authorities were rumours of miraculous occurrences swirling around the monk: that he would not get wet in the rain or could walk on water.

For the authorities this troublesome monk brought a combination of offences: outright political dissent and a spiritual one. Each time he was reprimanded by the authorities or ordered to the capital his reputation grew with my grandparents and many other supporters who took inspiration from his defiant stance. Ultimately Khruba Siwichai's detention in Bangkok would end after he agreed to accept the authority of the Council, but, for the government, resistance against centralised control in matters of religion and belief would recur in countless ways.

*

In the brief time I spent as a novice monk at a Bangkok temple I unwittingly bore witness to another disruptive episode in Thai Buddhism. I was in my first year at an American high school when my relatives suggested that I shave my head and undergo the ordination ceremony considered a rite of passage for many young Thai males. Of course, I didn't want to do it – I would be without my bass-heavy music and comfortable trainers – but family pressure won, as my participation would allow them to 'hold on to my yellow robes to reach heaven'. After taking my vows and chanting in Pali, I spent two weeks at the temple where my grandmother was a respected early donor.

Of all the temples in Bangkok, I found that this wasn't the worst place to be for a young Thai who'd lived half his life overseas. Compared to other temples, its modern chapel and verdant grounds were clean and well maintained. The small *kuti* where I'd sleep and meditate couldn't have been more than a few years old, with lacquered floorboards free from dust and mosquito nets without holes. After bathing and breakfast I devoted mornings and early afternoons to meditation with the guidance of older monks in a serene, simple hall. Over three decades ago the northern outskirts of Bangkok were not as built up with condominiums and malls, and sometimes, after the heat of the sun became bearable, I'd hop on a bicycle and ride across what seemed like endless fields in a lost idyll.

Opposite top: Buddhists paying respect to the Buddha on Vesak at Wat Phra Dhammakaya.
Opposite bottom: Novices releasing sky lanterns during the Yi Peng Festival in Wat Phantao, Chiang Mai. Yi Peng is a religious festival celebrated on the full moon of the lunar calendar in November in the north of Thailand. People gather to honour the Buddha and ask for good luck and wisdom.

Once we even had the chance to meet the abbot. I don't remember the conversation well – mostly small talk and his asking about our progress with meditation. Bespectacled and pale, Phra Chaiboon Dhammachayo looked young for an abbot. If he wasn't a monk with a shaved head, I thought, he could have passed for a doctor or accountant. I could not have known that a few decades later he would become a fugitive.

Wat Phra Dhammakaya was established in 1970 as an offshoot temple founded on the teachings of a famous Mahanikaya monk. The sect advocates the attainment of a state of *dhammakaya*, or body of enlightenment, as made possible through the sense of peace gained from its meditative techniques. As a novice I practised them every day, seated in a cross-legged lotus position. I pictured a crystal ball hovering just above my navel as I breathed deeply and chanted a simple Pali phrase. After my time as a monk I intermittently kept up with meditation, but my personal beliefs went in a more secular, agnostic direction. I didn't become a true believer of any official religion, but over the decades I continued to hear about Wat Dhammakaya and Phra Dhammachayo through relatives and Thai newspaper headlines.

I would not recognise the temple grounds were I ever to revisit them. The temple has grown vastly and is said to be the largest in the world, with its landholdings north of Bangkok having expanded from the original thirty-one hectares to at least 324. In addition to the spartan buildings familiar to me, many grander edifices were built, including a golden-domed, UFO-shaped cetiya containing over 300,000 life-size Buddha images and large enough to admit a

Higher Powers

Top: Wat Suan Dok, founded in 1370, is home to one of the two Buddha relics from the Sukhothai kingdom.
Bottom: Monks chanting before eating from their alms bowls at Wat Pa Ratchadaram, Lumphun province.

crowd of more than 150,000. Anywhere from 2,000 to 3,000 monks now live in the expanded temple complex and its more than 150 buildings. Outside the country the temple runs over a hundred meditation centres in thirty-four countries, from Milan to Kathmandu.

This infrastructural growth would not be possible without the Dhammakaya sect having gained hundreds of thousands of followers. Although the temple was first founded mainly with support from Bangkok's establishment, it met with even greater enthusiasm from the growing urban middle class. Its architectural expansion, which cost almost thirty-six billion baht (just over $1 billion) in construction costs, was paid for by donations that flowed in from a demographic disillusioned with traditional Buddhism and its didactic, archaic rules. Instead of proposing detachment from worldly objects and activities as a goal, the Dhammakaya sect not only promotes greater engagement it also promises a path to a truer self. To a rising middle class the promise must have seemed more appealing than the disavowal of newly acquired comforts and a positive trajectory of spiritual self-improvement more easily compared to desirable advancement in one's career. Much merit, to be enjoyed in this life or the next, would be attained by opening one's wallet. The temple's donation boxes were even labelled as an 'entrance to heaven'.

To critics, however, the idea that 'the more merit you make, the more you gain' sounded not so dissimilar to a promissory statement from an investment firm. The view that the temple represented the mass commercialisation of Buddhism, along with the extravagance of its construction projects, led religious purists to accuse the temple and its abbot of materialism contrary to the teachings of the Buddha and to compare its fundraising practices to direct marketing, with bonus incentives to be paid in the afterlife. Also appalling to some were claims of miraculous occurrences at the temple, including visions of a monk superimposed on the sun above its domed hall, as well as Dhammakaya lore that went beyond traditional teachings to describe a cosmic fight between the forces of light and darkness, one that might not feel out of place in a Hollywood film franchise.

These unorthodox beliefs would prove to be too much for the tolerance of the official religious authorities. In 1999 the supreme patriarch of the Sangha Supreme Council recommended the disrobement of Phra Dhammachayo, who had been facing charges of embezzlement. Cases against him were dropped by the government in August 2006, leading some critics to speculate he'd been helped by Prime Minister Thaksin Shinawatra, also a popular figure with a large swathe of middle-class Thais. The association between the populist politics of the Shinawatra clan and Dhammakaya ensured that the sect would be disfavoured by an establishment class already wary of its new spin on Thai Buddhism.

Any unofficial alliance would be short-lived, as a *coup d'état* the following month removed Shinawatra from office, and his sister Yingluck, later elected prime minister, would face the same fate a few years on. In 2015 the Department of Special Investigation found that 1.4 billion baht ($39 million) had been donated to the temple by the embezzler of a collapsed credit union. The discovery refuelled the prior cases

THE 'LITTLE WAR'

To the Thais it is Phra Viharn, and to the Khmer, Preah Vihear. This 11th-century temple dedicated to the god Shiva is perched on a rocky outcrop on the border between Thailand and Cambodia. It is the symbol of a centuries-old rivalry, fuelled by a number of different cultural disputes. (Take martial arts, for example: what the Thais call Muay Thai is Kun Khmer to the Cambodians.) Even though the temple had long been within Thailand's territory, in 1962 the International Court of Justice assigned it to Cambodia based on the borders drawn up by the French in 1904. In July 2008 it was listed as a World Heritage Site. A 'little war' broke out over its control, ending in 2011 when Yingluck Shinawatra became the Thai prime minister, helped by the fact that her brother Thaksin was politically aligned with his Cambodian counterpart Hun Sen. This special relationship resumed in 2023 when a coalition led by Thaksin's Pheu Thai party won the elections. The reconciliation was confirmed on 7 February 2024 with a meeting between the then Thai premier Srettha Thavisin and Hun Sen's son Hun Manet, who led the Cambodian forces in the little war of 2008. So it seems that a status quo has been reached at Preah Vihear/Phra Viharn and, more importantly, a programme of cooperation established for the future exploitation of an area of the Gulf of Thailand believed to contain a deposit of 311 billion cubic metres of natural gas. But these agreements have come at a cost to human rights: both countries committed not to give refuge to each other's dissidents. (Massimo Morello)

and sentiments against the temple in conservative circles, even leading to in-fighting within the Sangha Supreme Council itself when a senior monk with ties to the Dhammakaya temple was blocked from ascension to supreme patriarch following a scandal involving a vintage Mercedes-Benz. Then in 2017 the government attempted to arrest the infamous Dhammakaya abbot. More than four thousand police officers surrounded the temple, facing off defiant crowds of monks and lay followers. The siege lasted twenty-three days before the authorities ended their search. The abbot was nowhere to be found.

As of today, the whereabouts of the now defrocked Dhammachayo is still unknown. I've heard rumours of him having escaped the country and staying elusive and surgically disguised in the Middle East. Some Dhammakaya faithful would laugh at the suggestion. According to whispers in their circles the former abbot had never left the temple grounds. Protected by the supernatural abilities of his advanced spiritual state, they say, he's still there but unseen, biding his time until the right moment for his return.

*

It's not easy to be a religious firebrand, but it may be as hard to be a true Buddhist by official standards.

When Buddhism arrived in Thailand it did not find a place devoid of beliefs. Indigenous animist faiths and an abundance of shamanistic rituals existed throughout the region, and the introduction of larger, more organised religions never fully replaced them. As the migration of people, goods and ideas from the Indian subcontinent continued over centuries, Hinduism

became integrated into a kind of Hindu-Buddhist worship long adopted by the lowest to highest rungs of Thai society. While the Siamese state has long favoured Buddhism it has necessarily allowed room for other religious views, dating back to the days of the Ayutthaya kingdom when Muslims and Roman Catholics were largely allowed freedom to practise and preach. Siamese religious openness and tolerance allowed for profitable trade with foreign powers, both European and Asian, and created a cosmopolitan society with influences from all directions. It should come as no surprise that the forms of Buddhism practised by many ordinary Thais usually deviate far from purist doctrine.

One evening I visited my cousin Pravee to take a look at his home altar. At the centre of its topmost shelf, traditional Thai statuettes of the Buddha sat serenely in their closed-eyed, lotus position next to a bouquet of artificial flowers. They were joined by many others all around them: another Buddha in the Japanese Shinto style, giants from the *Ramakien* saga – the Thai rendition of India's *Ramayana* tale – standing guard like the statues at Bangkok's Grand Palace, and statuettes of Ganesh and Vishnu. Beside them were figures representing Nagas, the serpent deities, and on a nearby table stood figurines of small boys believed to hold the mischievous spirits of children who work in miraculous ways to benefit their keepers.

'But not any more,' cousin Pravee said. 'These kids here have received enough merit to move on to their next lives.' He counts himself a believer of *mu*, or *mutelu*, a recently coined name for the use of auspicious artefacts and occult rituals in order to improve one's life circumstances. A recent corporate survey showed that 75 per cent of Thais believe in some form of *mutelu*, from seeking religious relics and making merit at temples for good luck to fortune telling and numerology.

Despite the new descriptive term, the phenomenon is not new, and it can be hard to discern a line between organised religion and supernatural folk beliefs. For generations Thais who believe in supernatural powers have sought magical objects or tattooed themselves with squiggly patterns and phrases said to offer divine protection. Many wear amulets decorated with images of the Buddha or famous monks, with some highly desirable amulets fetching fifty million baht ($1.4 million). A visitor to any well-funded Thai temple is likely to encounter opportunities to acquire – or, to use the common euphemistic term, 'rent' – such celebrated items. One can also make merit for karmic prosperity and luck, in this life or any future ones, by feeding the fish in the temple's canal or helping to pay the temple's utility bills.

As a cultural trend, *mutelu* repackages

and expands a Thai catalogue of belief-driven products and services. It piggybacks on existing religious practices and updates them for a more industrialised, hyper-capitalist society, with competitive edge to its believer as the major selling point. My cousin described the portmanteau 'muketing' now popular in his line of work – property sales. As part of the sales process customers increasingly demand that houses have the right blend of favourable traits for their personal economic wellbeing, from the right master-approved feng shui to the property having been properly blessed by monks. At many development sites my cousin is usually the one with incense sticks and flowers in hand, helping lead his team in prayer to the Buddha, as well as the one performing necessary ceremonies to appease discontented spirits and seek the kindness of higher deities.

I asked my cousin if he felt any contradiction between the philosophy of detachment proposed by traditional Thai Buddhism and the request for personal success through supernatural means.

'The abstract ideal doesn't always fit real life,' he answered. 'People need something to believe in that can help them survive and prosper, so temples can also survive and prosper.'

Perhaps that is why there is not only tolerance of *mutelu* by the establishment but also advocacy. Corporations, from banks to online platforms, have seized on those beliefs to promote their businesses to consumers, offering digital fortune-telling and ways of making merit with temples via apps. Because Thai-style *mutelu* has also gained popularity overseas, as seen with Chinese tourists who regularly crowd the Brahman-Buddhist Erawan Shrine in the heart of Bangkok, both the Tourism

> 'As much as the state religious apparatus has tried to shape Thai Buddhism with its goal of fidelity to Pali texts and adherence to strict codes of conduct, can it ever govern what millions believe and practise in their actual daily lives?'

Authority and Ministry of Commerce have promoted *mutelu* tourism as a revenue stream.

But tolerance and support aren't always guaranteed. Not far from where my family lives, followers of a peculiar deity erected a statue in front of a hotel on a busy intersection in Bangkok. Called Kru Kai Kaew, or glass-bodied teacher – a representation of an ancient Khmer sorcerer – the statue depicted a gaunt, gargoyle-like figure seated in a lotus position similar to that of other Buddha or monk sculptures, but its colour was entirely black save for gilded fangs extending over the lips and long fingernails painted red. Followers of this mythical guru believed offerings to the statues could grant them protection and winning lottery numbers.

Major Thai news sources latched on to the spectacle, with regular coverage of fortune seekers and sound bites from curious passers-by at the intersection. Rumours soon circulated on social media that the worship of Kru Gai Gaew necessitated the sacrifice of puppies or kittens. A civic group accredited by the Religious Affairs Department protested against the statue's installation, citing fear by the local populace that it promoted devil worship, and another asked Bangkok's governor to remove the statue, declaring that it went against appropriate religious norms.

The state would have the ultimate say. The last time I passed by the intersection the statue was no longer there. At the end of 2023 it was removed by order of the State Railway of Thailand, which had leased the land to the hotel, with a fine to the hotel of 1.3 million baht ($36,400). Some threshold of permissible deviation from official standards had been crossed, and a show of authority needed to be made for the millions following the news. But will it work? As much as the state religious apparatus has tried to shape Thai Buddhism with its goal of fidelity to Pali texts and adherence to strict codes of conduct, can it ever govern what millions believe and practise in their actual daily lives?

I recently ran into Uncle Jumpol. He'd made it a personal tradition each birthday to drive up north to visit a former temple of Khruba Siwichai in Lamphum, and I asked him how his meditation sessions went.

'What meditation sessions?'

'Don't you go up there to perform dharma rites?'

'That's for the monks,' said my uncle, always one for jokes. 'I help feed them in the morning, so they can make merit on my behalf. That's the only way I'll get to heaven.'

Generational Trauma in Thailand's Deep South

VEERAPONG SOONTORNCHATTRAWAT

Translated by Noh Anothai

Students in class at Maahad Darul Maarif School in Pattani province. The school – which was founded by Haji Sulong Abdulkadir al-Fatani, a reformer and separatist in Pattani who was opposed to the nationalist concept of Thainess – has been suspected by the Thai authorities of being a place where separatist ideology is cultivated.

In the three Malay-majority provinces in Southern Thailand the civilian population finds itself a double target – for armed separatist groups as well as repression on the part of central government – creating a spiral of traumas that are passed down from one generation to the next. Reporting from the heart of Pattani province, a journalist meets some of the people who are trying to stop the cycle of violence.

We are travelling on the Pattani–Narathiwat Highway on our way to Tak Bai in Thailand's Deep South. The imposing ruins of the Krue Se Mosque can be seen from the road, and the traveller in me is fascinated by the ancient brick structure and its Gothic-Islamic architecture.

'It's beautiful,' I say, but Abdullah Ngoh breaks the spell, pointing out the reality that each shattered brick records a history of pain.

'Most people think so,' he responds, 'but I don't care much for architecture.' He peers at the mosque through the rear-view mirror as we continue along the road. His direct manner somehow makes his remarks sound less pointed. 'Whoever wants to rebuild the mosque can go ahead,' he continues, 'but I'd rather restore justice. That's what's important for us right now.'

The matter of justice is what lies at the heart of the conflict that for two decades, since 2004, has blighted the three provinces – Pattani, Yala and Narathiwat – that abut Thailand's southern border with Malaysia. Just like at the epicentre of an earthquake, here people's lives have been shaken apart – here, where special laws imposed by central government pass down trauma from generation to generation and from the dead to the living.

HISTORICAL TRAUMAS

Since the Pattani region was annexed by the Thai state during the reign of King Rama V (reigned 1868–1910), a liberation movement – by turns both peaceful and violent – has called for independence and the right to self-governance for the local Malay majority. Despite documents produced by the Thai administration in the early 19th century referring to the inhabitants of the newly incorporated Pattani sultanate as 'Malays' or *khaek* – a Thai term for people of perceived Hindu or Muslim identity that also means 'guest' – for the sake of nation-building, a policy of national integration was implemented, one that called inevitably for Malays to be transformed into Thais in their own homeland. Their ethnic identity – their language, clothing, education, history and culture – was placed under the state's rigid control in 1938, and that is how it remains to this day. Anyone who even wears traditional Malay clothing can be stopped and subjected to scrutiny by one of the officers stationed on every street corner in the three southernmost provinces.

The murder of prominent Malay religious leader Haji Sulong Abdulkadir after the Second World War still casts a long shadow. The imam and activist was arrested in 1948 for treason after having championed Malay rights during

VEERAPONG SOONTORNCHATTRAWAT is a freelance writer whose work explores social issues through the experiences of individuals. He focuses on human interest stories, particularly the effects of historical and social conflicts. His writing, both fiction and non-fiction, has been published in books, magazines and by news agencies.

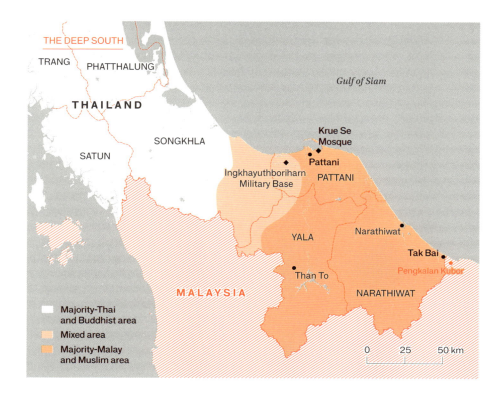

the dictatorship of Field Marshal Plaek Phibunsongkhram, a proponent of cultural assimilation. In August 1954 Haji Sulong Abdulkadir mysteriously disappeared along with some of his followers while he was being transported to court. This marked a turning point in the region's history, with the emergence between the sixties and eighties of numerous separatist groups, such as PULO (from the English acronym Pattani United Liberation Organisation) and the National Revolutionary Front (or BRN, the Barisan Revolusi Nasional), who fought for the liberation of a 'Malay Pattani'. According to scholars, in those decades the Thai administration had little thought for either human rights or for the decentralisation of power and so governed the region with force.

Political scientist Muhammad Ilyas Yaprang, from Ramkhamhaeng University in Bangkok, explains that the development of the independence movement – initially nationalist in nature – must be read in the international context characterised by the Islamic Revolution in Iran in 1979. In the last decade there has been much less appetite for an Islamic state, and democratic ideas of political participation, accountability of governments and transparency have taken hold in the region. 'The idea of an independent Islamic state is no longer conceivable today,' says the scholar. The solution to the conflict, he says, is the creation of a sense of national belonging, and the priority must be to draft a new constitution, underlining how the situation of the Malay majority and other ethnic

TWENTY YEARS OF VIOLENCE

The NGO Deep South Watch, which monitors the conflict in the southernmost provinces of Thailand, has recorded 21,485 'incidents' (including bombings, armed clashes, shootings, arson, attacks, disorder, searches and arrests) between the start of 2004 and March 2022 (the most recent data available).

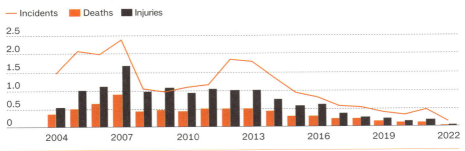

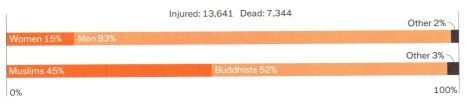

SOURCE: DEEPSOUTHWATCH.ORG

MAKING PEACE WITH THE GHOSTS

As with the chicken and the egg, it is not always clear what the cause-and-effect relationship is between insurrection and repression in the decades-long conflict in Thailand's Deep South. When the state seeks to reaffirm its control, the separatists target institutions and individuals seen as representatives of the authorities (army, police, civil servants, teachers and Buddhist monks), triggering a tough response from the government that provokes further attacks and further repression. Separatism is now so deeply rooted in society that, for the government, it is like 'confronting ghosts' (a common description). Even when they have attempted to engage in dialogue, the central authorities have struggled to find people to talk to; the various armed groups – the main one being the BRN – rarely take responsibility for any attacks, except when it is useful to them as a means of asserting their influence on the movement as a whole, which in reality is limited. In 2013, with mediation from Malaysia, where some insurrectionists take refuge, Yingluck Shinawatra's government began talks with the BRN, but immediately afterwards the military junta tried to create conflict within the separatist camp by engaging in dialogue with a number of other factions. Direct talks between the BRN and the government resumed in 2020, leading to brief ceasefires – which were not respected by those groups who were excluded. In spite of a resurgence of violence ahead of the 2023 elections, changes of government in both Thailand and Malaysia have given new impetus to the latest in a long series of attempts to bring peace to the region.

minorities in the three border provinces is inextricably linked to national politics.

TWO DECADES UNDER SPECIAL LAWS
The latest wave of violence began with the theft of 413 firearms from a military camp in the Cho-airong district of Narathiwat province in January 2004, during the government of Prime Minister Thaksin Shinawatra, followed by a clash between the perpetrators and military officials that is known as the Krue Se Mosque incident. Early in the morning of 28 April insurgents attacked several army bases and police checkpoints in the three provinces. There were 108 deaths, including five state agents and thirty-two militants, who were killed when the mosque in which they had taken refuge was surrounded and came under heavy fire.

In October of that same year police forcibly dispersed a gathering of Malay Muslims in the town of Tak Bai, causing seven deaths. Over 1,300 demonstrators were arrested and loaded on to military transport trucks to be transferred to a base in Pattani. Packed on these trucks like so many pieces of timber, seventy-eight died from suffocation en route. For both 'incidents' the statute of limitations ran out in 2024.

Since 2004 the Thai government has administered the three southern provinces as an 'extraordinary zone' through the promulgation of special laws – including an emergency decree and martial law – across the region. These regulations give the authorities complete freedom to search, arrest or even imprison any person 'suspected' of being involved in a public security case without having to initiate a criminal investigation or judicial proceedings as in normal situations. Furthermore, they almost completely close the channels for legal action or demanding restitution from the state, further complicating the defence of human rights in the region. Meanwhile, armed groups have continued to attack government and civilian targets in a number of ways, including bombings, shootings and arson, prompting yet more heavy-handed responses from the government. According to Deep South Watch, an NGO that monitors the conflict, the violence of the last two decades has resulted in the deaths of no fewer than 7,300 people and another 13,500 injured. Civilians – both Buddhist Thais and Muslim Malays – account for the majority of these.

*

While travelling through Tak Bai, I note that Abdullah spends a lot of time on his phone. If he's not driving, he's texting someone. When he finally puts his phone down he says to me, 'Two people were arrested today.'

Several days earlier I had visited Abdullah at the offices of JASAD, the organisation he founded to help victims of the special laws. The offices are located on the second storey of a building of the sort that was popular in the 1970s. I found him lying stretched out on the floor as if on a prayer mat; defending human rights in Pattani is exhausting work. 'Religion forbids us to give up hope,' he says, opening his eyes but not getting up, 'but sometimes our bodies are exhausted.'

Abdullah agreed to accompany me to Tak Bai on the morning of 24 October 2023 to participate in the commemoration of the nineteen-year-old tragedy. The ceremony would also serve as a call for justice because, although the statute of limitations on the Tak Bai incident was about to expire, none of the perpetrators had yet appeared in court.

'Do any songs have special meaning to you?' I ask Abdullah on the way.

'Yes, one does,' he replies. He remains silent for a moment, his hands gripping the steering wheel. 'There's one that means a lot to me.'

ROCK SONGS AND THE CALL TO PRAYER
Eighties rock arrived in Sai Buri, Abdullah's home town in Pattani province, via Malaysia.

Guns n' Roses crossed the border at Pengkalan Kubor without showing their passports. At Abdullah's house the guitars on Gary Moore's 'Still Got the Blues' were only turned down when the call to prayer rang out from the local mosque. But Abdullah's favourite band is Green Day.

'I don't consider myself a traditionalist,' he says.

In the early 2000s Abdullah moved to Bangkok to enrol at Ramkhamhaeng University, but instead of studying he spent his time selling used rock-band T-shirts while learning to repair mobile phones. With younger friends from Pattani, on Friday evenings he would take the bus to pubs on Khao San Road, the famous backpackers' district, to drink Coca-Cola or Fanta and listen to rock music.

'Our family is very religious,' explains Abdullah. 'I don't drink because it's not allowed, but I'm crazy about music.'

In those days the Thai government required telephone operators in the three southernmost provinces to register all prepaid SIM cards. Since 2004 detonating explosive devices using a phone had become a common terrorist technique. Having returned to his home town in 2006, Abdullah decided to open a little phone-repair shop in the market at Banang Sata in neighbouring Yala province. Around three years later he was summoned for questioning in line with the government's special laws. 'They wanted to know about my SIM cards,' he explains. The officers told him he would be in custody for seven days under the rules of martial law, and he left Yala for Narathiwat immediately. 'I even took my football boots with me,' he laughs at his own naivety, 'but in truth it was hell.'

As allowed by the emergency decree, Abdullah was eventually detained for thirty-five days.

'They showed me photos of so many people,' he recalls, but he didn't recognise any of them. Despite all the methods they used to coerce 'the truth' from him, none of his answers corresponded to what the officers wanted to hear.

'We'll kill you right here if you don't confess,' they threatened him.

At last, semi-conscious and gasping for air after the sack covering his head had been removed, Abdullah managed to gather his senses. 'At that moment I thought I wasn't ever going home,' he says.

Between 2009 and 2014 Abdullah was detained under the special laws three times, with serious psychological consequences. Re-experiencing trauma is a symptom of post-traumatic stress disorder (PTSD). Once triggered, memories of a bad event come back so vividly that it's like reliving the experience, and the mind can't think of anything else.

'After that first time I swore to myself that I would never go back,' he says. But he was detained again in 2012, this time for seven days. After his release he took out a loan from a bank to open a new phone-repair shop in Sai Buri, but every

Thai soldiers during a security check of local civilians on a road between Yala and Pattani. Since the 2004 uprising martial law has been imposed in three southern border provinces. Numerous civilians have been arrested, disappeared or extrajudicially killed by the Thai authorities, and the cities and roads are dotted with numerous checkpoints.

Generational Trauma in Thailand's Deep South

> 'At last, semi-conscious and gasping for air after the sack covering his head had been removed, Abdullah managed to gather his senses.'

time a bomb went off or another armed ambush took place, soldiers would surround his shop before marching in and destroying everything until customers no longer dared to show up.

'So I decided to run away.' He was thirty-one years old, and for a while he drifted from village to village, a stranger in his own land, doing any job he could find, whether mowing grass or harvesting rubber in the plantations. In 2014 he was served with yet another arrest warrant while he was hiding at a friend's house. He was arrested in May then released on bail while the prosecutor ordered the dismissal of his case.

With the help of national and international human rights organisations, Abdullah decided to found JASAD, a network for victims of the Thai government's special laws, building it out of his own painful memories. The group is made up of more than twenty volunteers who understand the special regulations well. They monitor detainees closely, visiting them at military bases and police stations. Physical abuse and torture often occur in the first thirty-seven days of detention – the seven days granted to the authorities under martial law plus thirty more by emergency decree – which the victims usually do not dare mention to visiting relatives for fear of repercussions once the latter have left.

'We understand the pain of those who have been wronged, of those who are far away from home. When no one comes to visit the sense of isolation is indescribable.' Therefore Abdullah encourages relatives to visit inmates every day. 'If there are travel expenses, we try to reimburse them.'

WE ALL SHARE THE SAME BODY

After the midday prayers Abdullah sits smoking a cigarette in front of his office. The pungent smell of tobacco has yet to fade before he opens the door and enters. There is a sticker depicting a lit candle on the door.

'We are all experts in detention here,' he says, introducing himself to the family of a detainee that had arrived from Narathiwat. It isn't a joke but rather a way of acknowledging their fears. A candle flame helps chase away both fear and the dark.

A few days before, one of their family members had been suspected of involvement two months earlier in an incident in Yarang district and had been taken in by the military. Now the family sits listening intently to Abdullah like students at a religious school. But his lesson – delivered completely in Malay – is not on the principles for a peaceful life but on the laws that have violated their rights for twenty years.

Although the right to legal representation is fundamental to the judicial process, this does not apply to suspects in Pattani. They are rarely given the opportunity to see or consult a lawyer. Interrogations and testimony are often conducted without the presence of legal representation or other trusted persons.

News outlets regularly report cases of torture in detention, sometimes even killings – even if the authorities deny it – and people are understandably afraid.

'If our brothers and sisters are hurt,' says Abdullah, 'each one of us is hurt, because as Muslims we share the same body.' Data collected by JASAD indicates that at least half of all prisoners require psychological care, as do their spouses, children and families, all of whom are affected indirectly. 'Nothing can ever go back to the way it was before,' he admits, 'just as it was for me.'

After citizens filed complaints with the National Commission on Human Rights between 2018 and 2019, security forces altered their preferred methods of torture in favour of those that leave no physical trace. One of the most degrading was when they would bring naked women into a cell who would then beg the male detainees to sleep with them – a form of sexual harassment designed to violate the latter's religious principles.

A law finally curbing the use of torture and forced disappearances in 2022 marked a major advance in the protection of human rights in Thailand. This law requires state officials responsible for any arrest to immediately report and catalogue the proceedings. Interrogations and searches must be recorded on video or audio until the suspect is turned over to investigators or released. According to Pornpen Kongkachonkiet, director of the Cross Cultural Foundation, in the two years between the start of the pandemic and the promulgation of the law alone there were at least ninety-two extrajudicial killings.

BIRDS AND CAGES

'Aren't you going to lock the car?' I ask Abdullah in surprise when we stop for coffee at a petrol station. He jokes that he doesn't plan on staying long. After our coffee we continue the journey in silence. I think we could use some music.

'So, which song is it that means a lot to you?' I ask.

'There is a song,' he says, then adds, 'but it's not a rock song,' pre-empting his answer as if embarrassed. 'It's by Taylor Swift. "Safe and Sound". Have you ever heard it?' A researcher suggested he listen to it after hearing what Abdullah had been through in detention, hoping it would help him. Now, perhaps without knowing it, Abdullah's work embodies the meaning of the lyrics of Swift's 2022 song, vowing to remain with those who find themselves awake in a nightmare: 'Just close your eyes / The sun is going down / You'll be alright / No one can hurt you now / Come morning light / You and I'll be safe and sound'.

Certain triggers can cause extreme discomfort for patients with PTSD. For Abdullah anything that suggests confinement can set him off: the sight of soldiers surrounding a house in his neighbourhood or arresting someone he knows can make the nightmares return. For him, the sound of metallic parts turning in a lock is no different from an explosion. 'Don't make me feel trapped,' he says. 'Don't lock me in a room from the outside. I'm serious about any kind of confinement.'

When we reach Narathiwat, Abdullah shows me around Tak Bai, which is close to the border between Thailand and Malaysia. Hanging from a wooden railing at the port on the Golok River there is a birdcage that immediately reminds him of the dark, rectangular room at the Ingkhayuthboriharn Army Base where he was detained fourteen years earlier. As

soon as he sees the bulbul locked inside, he feels the desire to free the bird. He's done this before – breeding competitive songbirds is a Malay tradition, and Abdullah once released a friend's valuable pet. 'He wouldn't talk to me for days,' he jokes, before turning serious again. 'I can't stand seeing animals in cages.'

From the Sankalakhiri Mountains the Golok River flows into the Gulf of Siam, marking the border between the Tak Bai checkpoint on the Thai side and that of Pengkalan Kubor, Kelantan State, Malaysia. This October afternoon people are crossing as usual. But there are almost no shops open in the market. The boats are all moored in the port. A ferryman sits smoking one cigarette after another. 'With the bombings no Malaysians make trips any more,' he claims, gesturing at the market, silent as a ghost town. 'The bombings destroyed the economy here. The Malaysians are afraid to come.'

We are three days away from the nineteenth anniversary of the Tak Bai massacre, and explosions and shootings have been reported at several checkpoints. 'Between September and October there was an increase in skirmishes,' Ruslan Muso, director of the local news agency Wartani, explains to me. 'They [the separatists] might be sending a

Above: Abdullah Ngoh – who was repeatedly arrested and tortured by the Thai military – has now dedicated his life to working as a human rights defender with the NGO JASAD, a network that helps people impacted by the special laws in the Deep South.
Opposite: Matyaki Matyasin sits by the window at which her husband was extrajudicially killed when Thai soldiers surrounded their house and gunned him down in the early hours of 5 July 2023.

message to the government about the Tak Bai massacre. One of the key players – former Prime Minister Thaksin – is returning to Thailand [after many years of self-imposed exile following the military coup of 2014]. But on Tak Bai they [the government] are silent, and the statute of limitations is about to expire.'

BIRDS AND PEOPLE
The riverside playground opposite the Tak Bai police station is different from the way it was on the same date nineteen years before. The slides, swings and other equipment have been removed. Only one sign stubbornly remains, a reminder that children once played here. The old police station across the street has been demolished and replaced with a new one.

More than fifty volunteers in yellow T-shirts and blue scarves are going up and down the riverside with cleaning equipment, as if they wanted to sweep away the wounds of history, here, where that ill-fated demonstration took place. On that morning seven people died in front of the police station, and another seventy-eight lost their lives while being transported, crowded together with 1,300 other arrested protesters aboard some twenty-five military vehicles, to the base at Ingkhayuthboriharn. An investigation established that they died of suffocation but offered no evidence to indicate that foul play had taken place. Now the case is closed, and no perpetrators can be brought to justice.

The victims' families found the courage to file a lawsuit and demand restitution against the government in Pattani's provincial court, but in the end only a reconciliatory settlement was reached between the parties. Legal experts, however, have stated that the reconciliation agreement does not constitute a reason to suspend criminal proceedings before the statute of limitations expires.

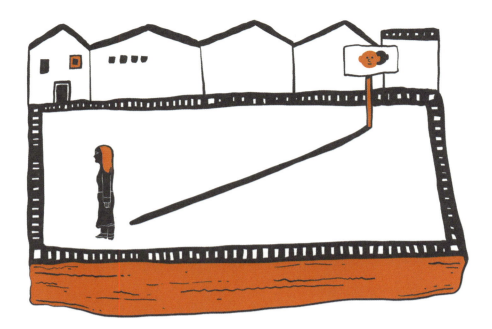

'I don't care about it any more. I'm old now,' confesses a Malay woman who lost her husband in the massacre. 'I don't want to fight in court. This year I'm fifty-eight.' I meet Kaya Mahama, the widow of Mahama Laobakor, one of the victims of the Tak Bai massacre, at De Lapae Artspace in Narathiwat, where she has brought a birdcage that belonged to her late husband to be displayed in an exhibition called *Listening to Silence: Remembering Tak Bai 2004*.

On the morning of 25 October Kaya had gone with her son to Tak Bai to purchase equipment for the mandatory military conscription he would be starting in a few days. Her husband had gone to a tea house as he did every morning. They left at home only their five birds hanging in wooden cages. That morning Kaya saw hundreds of demonstrators gathered in front of the police station in Tak Bai to demand the release of six people arrested during a search for weapons stolen from one of the army's depots. Although her son insisted they return home, Kaya was curious, and the two split up. Finally, police began to use water cannon to disperse the protesters; then there were gunshots, and everyone fell to the ground. It was then that Kaya found her husband. 'Come on!' he shouted. 'Let's get to the river!' Kaya threw herself on to her husband's back, and he began to crawl towards the playground and the riverbank beyond. People were being shot! Kaya turned and saw blood on someone's shirt. Officers were separating the women from the men and lining them up in front of the police station. The men were ordered to take off their shirts and, with their hands tied behind their backs, to crawl back to the street from the riverside. There they were piled into military vehicles like matchsticks in a box, one on top of the other – except these were human beings, not matches.

That evening some officers escorted Kaya home, but her heart remained in that playground. No one else returned home but her, so she passed the night alone, save for the five caged birds.

After her husband's death, while charges were brought against her husband's younger brothers and her son was serving in the military, an officer turned up at Kaya's door, as happened at the doors of many hundreds or even thousands of other households. 'I can't speak for the dead or tell you anything about what my husband was doing at the demonstration in the first place,' she told him. 'I can only speak for me and my son, because we had gone shopping together. Because my son was going to become a soldier.'

'Why did you allow your son to become a soldier? Why not let him be a rebel instead?' These were the words he had for a woman who had just lost her husband.

Kaya eventually sold the family farm and continued to live her life in fear. The birds in their cages still sang every morning, but for Kaya it was a song of sorrow, for while her husband was alive they would burst into song whenever he returned from the tea house. So one day she opened the cages, saying, 'Go on, we all have to fend for ourselves now. Your master is no longer here.' One after the other they each took flight, except for one. 'A white-breasted hen,' explains Kaya. 'It refused, so I gave it to my father. I didn't want to hear its song any longer. It reminds me of my husband.'

*

'I feel sick,' Abdullah tells me as we are returning to Pattani from Tak Bai. I offer to take his place at the wheel. He doesn't look good at all. He adjusts the seat and lies down. I want to put that Taylor Swift song on for him – and for Kaya and for everyone else who hasn't forgotten Tak Bai.

I only understand why Abdullah feels this way after learning that three months earlier he had witnessed another military operation in the area where he lived with his wife and children. Soldiers surrounded a house and took a man in for questioning, and Abdullah once again felt haunted by his past experiences. Restless, scared and unable to control his emotions, he feels in danger even when at home with his family.

'My psychiatrist told me to take medication for at least three months, but it made me drowsy and kept me from making important decisions, so I stopped,' says Abdullah. 'I've seen a lot of doctors. I've spoken with psychiatrists from Switzerland, India, Malaysia. They tell me when the wound is mental it's hard to go back to the way things were.'

We drive back to Pattani on the same highway along which, nineteen years earlier, those twenty-five trucks had transported both the living and the dead from Tak Bai to the Ingkhayuthboriharn Army Base.

PEACE TALKS

'They are what we call secondary victims,' the human rights activist Anchana Heemmina tells me several days later after hearing about my trip to Tak Bai. 'We often overlook those people, but they are the ones forced to live the rest of their lives in pain.'

I have arranged to meet Anchana at the coffee bar at Pattani's main hotel, but before I can start asking her questions, an uninvited guest approaches our table.

A LAND BRIDGE

The Kra Canal, which would connect the Andaman Sea to the Gulf of Thailand, cutting across the Kra Isthmus, the narrowest point in Southern Thailand – a distance of around forty kilometres, much shorter than either the Suez or Panama canals – was the dream of Narai the Great, king of Siam in the late 17th century. Since then the significance of the project has grown, as it would shorten the route between the Indian Ocean and the South China Sea, which carries around 30 per cent of global trade, by more than 1,100 kilometres. But in the meantime projected costs have risen to astronomical levels and, above all, the canal would risk becoming a symbolic line of separation between the three Malay Muslim-majority provinces in the south of Thailand and the rest of the country. The solution proposed when Srettha Thavisin was prime minister was a 'land bridge' consisting of a railway, motorway and pipelines, spanning around ninety kilometres across the Kra Isthmus between the ports of Ranong on the Andaman Sea and Chumpon on the Gulf of Thailand. Around twenty-five million containers each year would be offloaded from ships on one coast and be transported to the other side, where they would be loaded on to other ships to continue their voyage. This would shave approximately 15 per cent off the journey time. The forecast cost is in the region of $28 billion, which would have to be covered by international investments, and the largest investor would be the Chinese government. The bridge would solve the so-called 'Malacca Dilemma', in other words the need to transport goods and energy supplies via the chokepoint formed by the Malacca Strait and Singapore, a route controlled by the US navy. (M.M.)

'Are you Miss Anchana?' The man is tall and muscular; his hair is cropped. He wears a plaid shirt and trousers of a quick-drying fabric. A large chain hangs around his neck, and he has a thick jade ring on one finger.

'Yes, good afternoon,' replies Anchana. 'I'm not sure ...'

'It's about work,' he goes on, ignoring her and placing a chair beside me. 'Can I sit?'

At one in the afternoon the bar is empty except for us. The man introduces himself as an officer from the Conflict Resolution Centre with the Internal Security Operations Command (ISOC), a special unit of the Thai military tasked with maintaining national security in the Deep South.

'I've been wanting to meet you,' he tells Anchana. 'I've been wanting to meet and have a talk with you.'

'My schedule's rather full these days,' she replies.

'I've read your work. What particular business are we on today, dear?' He is probably trying to sound friendly, but it just comes across as patronising.

'An interview with a writer,' says Anchana, gesturing to me. 'And an interview with the EU.'

'And where are you from?' he asks me.

I explain to him that I'm there to do research for this article, but it's clear that he isn't interested in my work but rather in the woman seated across from both of us.

In January 2016 a report was published that exposed the systematic use of torture by government authorities against those suspected of threatening national security: *Report on Cases of Torture and Cruel, Inhuman or Degrading Treatment in the Southern Provinces (2014–2015)*. The authors were sued for defamation

by ISOC, although the lawsuit was later withdrawn. Anchana had worked with the Cross Cultural Foundation to compile the report, which is likely how she caught the attention of Big Brother.

'I've been doing this job for a long time,' the ISOC officer begins. 'I like listening to the next generation's ideas. What do you think? How do we bring peace back to the country?'

'Back … ?' Anchana repeats as if she's never heard the word before. 'And exactly when was the country at peace?'

'It was before, of course.'

'Before means different things to different people,' Anchana replies.

The officer's use of the word 'before' makes me think how history is used by both sides in a conflict to create a sense of legitimacy for their own political ends.

'Of course, we all have different identities,' the man replies. 'Buddhists, Muslims – you're Buddhist, aren't you?' This question is directed to me.

'Until there is an open dialogue with the separatist movement the issue will not be resolved,' replies Anchana as if testing the waters.

'We need to look at the roots of the conflict,' the other immediately replies but avoids elaborating. 'We first need to ask who makes up the movement. What is their goal?'

The grave of one of the victims of the 2004 Tak Bai incident; more than eighty demonstrators died when the military moved in on a crowd protesting against the detention of six men at a police station.

Generational Trauma in Thailand's Deep South

Opposite: A fisherman prepares his *kolae* for the next catch at the village pier in the Panare district of Pattani province. *Kolaes* are traditional fishing boats found in the Southern region of Thailand. They are decorated in a mix of Malay, Javanese and Thai styles.
Below, from left: A woman helps fishermen gather fish and shellfish from the net after landing the catch; students reviewing their studies before afternoon prayers; a boy squats next to a slaughtered cow, whose meat will be shared with the poor and throughout the community during the Muslim holiday of Hari Raya (Eid al-Fitr).

'And can you tell me what that is?' Anchana asks him his own question.

'In my own personal opinion,' he says, 'is it wrong to want Malay territory returned? My feeling is that it's not if it's for the sake of Malay identity.' He then gives a historical timeline of the conflict before returning to the legitimacy of the separatists' demands. 'If we go back about a thousand years, the people who walked this land practised animism, Hinduism and Buddhism then later adopted Islam. When you dig a little deeper and look into the past, we find a place where different cultures overlapped. We cannot deny these facts.' He speaks with caution, aware that his interlocutor might object if she found a hole in his logic. 'There was a Buddhist governor here,' he continues, probably referring to a time when the region was still called Langkasuka, before the Pattani Sultanate emerged around the 15th century. 'This governor was ill. He was treated by a Muslim doctor to whom he promised to embrace Islam

Generational Trauma in Thailand's Deep South

if he recovered. We cannot deny it: harmony has existed among us for a long time.'

His arguments are drawn from official Thai historiography, which links Buddhism to Thai identity to affirm the legitimacy of the central government, which, in turn, is celebrated as a reconciliatory force between different ethnic groups and religious identities. I am reminded of a reflection made by historians Michael J. Montesano and Patrick Jory in the book *Thai South and Malay North: Ethnic Interactions in the Plural Peninsula* (2008), where they observe that historically arguments against separatism involve turning the border, which is artificial and hypothetical, into something inviolable. Likewise, they write that claims for autonomy or special permissions based on ethnic or religious identities make what are essentially fluid and dynamic categories rigid and static.

'But in this situation, how do we talk to the people fighting?' Anchana's question brings me back to the conversation.

'Instead of using force, why don't we fight using the parliamentary system?' His proposal was intriguing. 'I studied the separatist movement in Quebec. Have you heard of it? I mean, if you have, I wouldn't want to preach to the choir ...'

The way that the movement for Quebecois independence in Canada has been dealt with has been cited as one example in which the application of the right to self-determination (RSD) has led to genuine solutions.

'Would it be possible to do the same here?'

'Would RSD be possible?' replies the soldier. 'There's a protocol, a series of steps, to implementing these things.'

'In any case,' says Anchana, 'why don't you stop the persecution of those Prince of Songkla University students?'

'That is not in my power,' he answers. 'I don't have the authority to do that.'

'Please stop the legal proceedings against the students,' Anya pleads.

A WOUND THAT RUNS THROUGH GENERATIONS

In late October 2023 I meet Sarif Saleman and Hayati Thoyeng, two of those students from Prince of Songkla University in Hat Yai to which Anchana was referring. They are preparing for mid-term exams while at the same time waiting to appear in court. The previous June Sarif and four other students were accused by the Region 4 Internal Security Operations Command of sedition, incitement to violence and belonging to a separatist group. Hayati had been called to testify.

It's incredible that such serious accusations had come out of a seminar they hosted on campus grounds. The seminar that day had seen the introduction of the National Student Movement (Pelajar Bangsa), but what probably exercised the authorities most was the informal referendum on this question: Do you agree that the 'right to self-determination' will allow the people of Pattani to legally gain independence?

'How did everyone vote that day?' I ask Hayati.

'We haven't counted the votes yet,' he replies. Everyone was in shock; no one had expected that a seminar and a new student organisation would have attracted so much attention from the Department of Public Safety.

'That day I read a poem on stage,' Sarif says. He had chosen lines from 'Tanah Air Yang Tercinta' ('My Birthplace') by an anonymous poet:

THAI HOSTAGES

In the eyes of the wider world it might be just a footnote to the tragic events in Israel on 7 October 2023 and the subsequent devastation of Gaza, but Thailand also paid a heavy toll that day: around forty Thais died in the attack and more than thirty were taken hostage, two dozen of whom were freed a month later but two died in captivity. On top of that, with a sizeable Muslim minority in the south sympathetic to the Palestinians, the tensions in the Middle East represent a significant headache for the Thai national government. In line with its policy of bamboo diplomacy (see the box on page 145), Thailand cooperates with Israel but does not support the transfer of the capital from Tel Aviv to Jerusalem, as backed by Donald Trump. It recognises the Palestinian state and maintains discreet relations with Iran as well. The Hamas attack revealed to the world the presence of Thai workers in Israel, who numbered around 30,000 before 7 October, even though in reality it is not a recent phenomenon. Since the 1990s many Thais have found employment in the Israeli agricultural sector, often through illegal recruitment schemes and with few rights – there are thought to have been 172 deaths as a result of poor working conditions during the 2010s. In the autumn of 2023 more than ten thousand immigrants were repatriated, but since then their numbers have returned to stability, and Israel would now like to employ them in construction as well. It is estimated that around 1.1 million Thais live abroad – not so many for a Southeast Asian country – with the largest communities to be found in the USA, South Korea, Australia, Taiwan and Germany.

Melayu [Malay] is my race
Fatoni [Pattani] is my land
Islam is my religion
This is who I am.

'We live under oppression,' he says, 'but poetry helps us become who we are.'

Here is a young man who has chosen to fight with poems invoking Pattani identity, an identity that has been erased by the Thai state by usurping the historical narrative. But history is itself a field on which people fight in order to legitimise their political aims. As long as no weapons are brandished, history is one battlefield governed by peaceful methods.

When I ask him what he thinks of the situation in Pattani, he replies, 'I feel like a target. The two players – the Thai state and the armed insurrection – throw darts to see who can score the most points. But it's the target who gets hurts most.'

'We would like to be part of the peace process,' adds Hayati, who had recently been summoned to testify in one case against Sarif, 'but it seems that this door is closed to people like us. RSD helps us see more solutions. The people here can determine their own fates and what they want out of life.'

Sarif and Hayati were born in 2002, so they grew up with checkpoints on the roads. Everywhere they have been they have seen wanted signs and arrest warrants at intersections next to posters showing smiling army officials and police officers shaking hands with local religious leaders.

Hayati's father was the head of a village in Than To district, Yala province, in a so-called 'red zone' where armed separatist groups are still active. For as long as she can remember Hayati accompanied her father on visits to members of the community who had been arrested and imprisoned. 'I was also with him in Bo Thong prison in the Ingkhayuthboriharn Army Base,' she recalls, naming places where no one would ever want to go.

Hayati had dashed her village's hopes by choosing to study at university instead of attending a religious school. The community would have preferred her to become a religious instructor rather than a hard-nosed human rights activist. 'But this is the society I grew up in,' says Hayati, referring to the ubiquity of the two armed factions. Her people's lives are like those of prisoners of war held hostage by special laws in exchange for a fake peace.

When she was in her final year at high school a government drone flew over the grounds of her religious school. A number of emotions seized Hayati then: both bewilderment at what officials could have been wanting to achieve and an outrage that rooted itself deep within her. 'At the time we were bathing. I felt like I had been violated. I tried to complain to our school administrators, but they said we had not been the only school.' After a while, the matter was forgotten.

The passage of time eventually brings amazing things to pass, things that turn out to be extremely common. Hayati's father passed into the mercy of Allah, and she fell from his arms to become the adult she is today. Villagers who had been imprisoned without reason in her youth were released after many years. 'Some had been in prison for seven years, and when they were released saw me for the first time as an adult. For me, time continued to flow; for them it had vanished into thin air, as it had for so many people.'

Hayati remembers that when she was a child fugitives would hide in their village. Her father always harboured them. She had been too young to understand why. 'If they really are innocent, why don't they just report to the police?' she had asked. 'As I grew up my perspective changed. We know they use torture, we know about the injustices. No wonder they fled and didn't want to collaborate with the state.'

The memory of Hayati's generation is built on the wounds of Abdullah's generation, while the fate of Abdullah's generation is an inheritance from Haji Sulong's like a wound that never heals. It is passed down like genes from one generation to the next. As long as 'justice' is merely a word for people to invoke in their darkest moments, there will always be those who get up to fight in any way they can.

'But my experiences,' says Hayati, 'have made me determined to protect my people through peaceful means.' 🐦

The central mosque in Pattani is crowded on Hari Raya. A hugely important day of tradition and celebration for Muslims worldwide, it is an occasion to be with family and honour Allah.

Heartland

Off the tourist trail and often looked down upon by Bangkok, every so often Thailand's Northeast comes back into fashion. From K-pop to MasterChef, everyone is talking about Isan just now, but the story told from outside is one of nostalgia and full of stubborn stereotypes.

PEERA SONGKÜNNATHAM

Rockets shoot into the sky at the Bun Bang Fai festival, the rocket festival in Yasothon, Northeastern Thailand. The main purpose of this folk tradition – found in the provinces of Yasothon, Kalasin and Roi Et – is to pay homage to Phaya Thaen, the god of rain, and ensure a good monsoon in that drought-prone region.

Isan is a large and populous region of Thailand that is traditionally a source of jasmine rice, manual labour and rural nostalgia to the rest of the country as well as to other, wealthier parts of the world – the factories of Taiwan, the kibbutzim of Israel, the berry woods of Scandinavia. One-third of the area, one-third of the population, Isan occupies no less than that in the Thai national imagination. The name, which literally translates as 'northeast', has come to mean so much more. Like the Brazilian Northeast, the Thai Northeast region has been painted in too-broad brush strokes as an arid and resource-poor region, so much so that a popular saying has arisen that goes, 'Whoever says Isan is arid, I'll take them by the hand to the Mekong flowing and sloshing. How can that be arid?'

Originally imposed by an absolutist regime in Bangkok around the turn of the 20th century, the name Isan, which was intended to replace and erase the ethnonym Lao, has become a pan-ethnic term of identity. Long denigrated for the Lao influences in its language and culture – in Thai slang, *lao* remains in use as a derogatory way of saying 'out of style' – every now and then 'Isan-ness' becomes hip. Strong-smelling fermented fish, arguably *the* quintessential Lao food ingredient, has had a long arc from unhygienic and unacceptable in polite society to part and parcel of Thai cuisine worthy of a feature on *MasterChef Thailand*. Isan Lao words and inflections that we've been taught for generations to purge from our speech – and for which schoolchildren used to be fined – now filter into the latest Thai slang via TikTok videos. Like Brazilian *nordestinos*, Thai northeasterners have, for a few generations now, reclaimed the region's name as a way to redefine the racist and classist stereotypes, which range from comical country bumpkins (see, for example, the trans fashion icon featured in *Time* magazine who makes runway-ready dresses out of chicken coops and hessian sacks!), uncultured urban transplants (visit the small-town café run by the winner of the 2017 Espresso Italiano Champion competition in Milan; he also serves sugarcane juice freshly squeezed from the crops in his father's fields!) to uninformed, easily influenced voters (do some ethnographic fieldwork in a village grocery store where 'boomers' gather for rounds of 40 per cent ABV rice whisky and political discussions – both matters of local pride!).

While most foreign travellers never set foot in the region, heading straight to the beaches and the islands of the south and the east, the alluring mountains of the

PEERA SONGKÜNNATHAM is a literary translator who was born and raised in Sisaket, Isan (1992–2007), worked as a journalist in Khon Kaen (2016–17) and has an empty house in Ubon Ratchathani. Peera lives in Indiana, USA.

THE GREAT MIGRATION

Almost a quarter of Bangkok's population is of Isan origin. During the first century of the city's history, however, the urban proletariat were mainly of Chinese heritage, until Mao took power in China in 1949, cutting off the migration routes. This, along with the Thai military's attempts to 'nationalise' the economy, created an immense demand for local labour. At that time, however, income in Isan, based mainly on exports of agricultural products to China, was much higher than that of the urban workforce, and the military government led by Plaek Phibunsongkhram adopted new policies, which still apply today, to force the rural masses of Isan to move to Bangkok. In 1955 it introduced a tax on rice exports that would revolutionise the relationship between the capital and Isan, the structure of the Thai economy and the labour market, which led to three significant effects: the value of rural production fell, forcing many peasants to move to the city; by lowering the price of rice, and therefore of labour, the policy supplied Thai industry with manpower at rock-bottom prices; and, finally, the proceeds of the tax were invested to support Bangkok's industrial growth rather than in the rural areas from which it came. This expropriation of human, agricultural and economic resources from the villages sparked the nation's industrial boom and forced millions of workers from Isan to join the labour force in Bangkok, where they remain to this day. (C.S.)

north or the temples and shopping malls of Central Thailand, chances are that many Thais with whom they come into contact – taxi drivers, street hawkers, restaurateurs – will hail from the northeastern plateau. Rather than being a cultural backwater, the Northeast is better understood as a cosmopolitan place that disrupts mainstream Thai cultural hierarchies. The US war in Vietnam, for example, brought temporary US military bases, a boom in prostitution and an enduring receptiveness to Westerners. Walking around the shopping malls of an Isan city nowadays, a sanctimonious civil servant might look with disapproval or envy at a dark-skinned, flat-nosed woman (classic 'Lao-faced') walking arm in arm with her white European retiree husband. 'Good for her!' I say – or, as we put it in Isan, *wassana hee baramee khuay* (she's among the fortunate ones with blessed pussies and meritful cocks). As Thailand struggles to get out of the middle-income trap, a problem obsessed over by economists and policy-makers, international love offers us a reprieve. Just as Thailand is a great country for foreigners to visit but not necessarily a good place in which to live, Isan is a great place for natives to return to after we find success but decidedly not a good place in which to be stuck.

As working-class Isan people move up the social ladder, replaced en masse by migrants from Myanmar – especially the underpaid maids and restaurant workers – Isan itself is undergoing a facelift. Take the example of Buriram, a province bordering Cambodia with a Khmer-speaking population and ancient Khmer ruins. During the 2010s this 'middle-of-nowhere' province reinvented itself as a sports destination with a motorcycle racing circuit – redirecting wayward youths from the night-time streets to the racetrack. Buildings in the provincial capital were forcibly repainted navy blue, the colour of the Buriram United Football Club, which has become the highest-grossing sports team in the country (although still running at a loss).

Back in the 2000s, in a blog post about 'negging', a male expat coaching other male expats in Thailand found it illustrative to talk about approaching a woman at a bar and saying 'You're beautiful. Are you from Buriram?' to catch her off guard with your backhanded compliment, and thus, theoretically, sparking her interest in you. But now everybody knows that Lisa of the K-pop girl group Blackpink, among the most famous pop stars in the world today, hails from Buriram. She's not treated as an exception to the rule either, now that nose jobs and skin-lightening opportunities have become readily accessible to the average Isan woman.

*

It is not only the urban elite who compete for investment into their respective provinces; many rural owner-operators of small farms also aspire to becoming capitalists in their own right. In tandem with our openness to Westerners is our aspiration for Chinese-style capital accumulation. In the early 20th century Chinese merchants started to appear in the region's towns and villages, often from Bangkok on the recently constructed railway; in time the term for a Chinese person in the Isan Lao language became synonymous with the word for merchant. While a pejorative elsewhere in Thailand, the word *jek*, derived from the Teochew term for the number one, is embraced by many non-Chinese Isan farmers who turn themselves into middlemen, merchants and entrepreneurs. Regardless of ethnicity, you can become a *jek* in Isan, and that's usually a better thing than being at the bottom of the agricultural supply chain, subject to the caprices of the climate and of middlemen.

This reality of the region's majority flies in the face of any romantic notions of Isan as the 'hearth' of peasant culture on one hand and as the hotbed of political revolution on the other. Leftist and left-leaning Thai intellectuals like to recall the history of communist insurrections in the region's mountains between the late 1950s and early 1980s. A poorly phrased speech in praise of Isan people as fighters for democracy is instructive. In 2018, during the lead-up to the first general elections since the 2014 *coup d'état*, the then secretary-general of the Future Forward Party, Piyabutr Saengkanokkul, juxtaposed negative Isan stereotypes with the

Opposite from top: Uncle Sai collects his cow after allowing it to roam free in his rice field during a drought in Roi Et in Isan; fisherman Supol Khamthong with his catch of a five-kilo black-eared catfish in Nong Khai; a farmer in Khon Kaen province connects a water pipe to divert water from other fields to hers, as the reservoir has dried up following a drought.

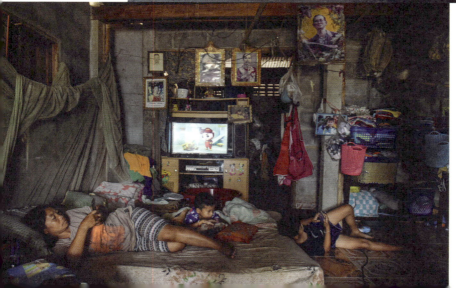

heroism of local socialist-politicians-turned-martyrs in the 1950s, aligning his new party with the latter to suggest that Isan people should know better than to vote for politicians who kowtow to coup-makers and big capitalists. The line that touched a raw nerve online could be translated as either 'Isan people are made to believe that they are clowns, manual labourers and people without knowledge' or 'Isan people are believed to be buffoons, manual labourers and uneducated'. The passive sentence structure makes it ambiguous as to who 'believes' these ideas. The former suggests mere misrepresentation; the latter, an accusation of internalised racism. Regardless of one's interpretation, the mere mention of such beliefs is already condescending enough for some. Did this guy think we're so ignorant that we don't know how we are seen by others in Thai society? For those who hadn't heard some of the things listed, let alone internalised them, reading the speech felt like receiving fresh insults. Me, a clown, too, not just an ignoramus? Me, a sucker for bad politicians?

It's fun to pick apart outsiders' reductive remarks about a region of more than twenty million people, but more insight can be gained by shining that same critical light on insiders' wounded pride. For this case also hints at the Isan people's attachment to an unimpeachably autonomous Isan identity – which is an impossibility from the start, as the term Isan literally defines the region by its location relative to Bangkok. Without Bangkok, Isan as we know it wouldn't exist. (However, the reverse is probably more true: without Isan, Bangkok as we know it wouldn't actually exist.) The problems surrounding the term have vexed regional intellectuals for generations. Unlike the 'Southern Borderlands' (incidentally, another Thai term defining a region by its location relative to Bangkok, but this time for the Muslim-majority provinces on the Malay Peninsula), where desires for some form of autonomy or sovereignty have long been accompanied by political demands or insurgent attacks, separatist strains of thought in the Northeast have mostly remained exactly that: strains of thought. Many peasant rebellions around the turn of the 20th century did try to break away, but they were crushed absolutely by the Siamese monarchy and also the French Empire on the other side of the Mekong. Disgruntled by Siam's new policies of administrative centralisation, disempowered local lords and commoners rallied around charismatic figures – men and women, monks and musicians – who called themselves 'meritful persons' and who prophesied the end of times. These millenarian

Opposite from top: Women in traditional Isan dress preparing to perform folk dances at the team competition of the Bun Bang Fai festival in Yasothon – they have won the title five times in a row; locals visiting Bang Fai, where the homemade rockets are decorated with gold-plated engravings and a great Naga, a half-human half-snake deity in Buddhist tradition; Pisamai Ruankham, a street vendor, comes from a family of fishermen, but the negative impact of dams built upstream has forced her family to find other ways of making a living.

HEALTHCARE FOR ALL

Life expectancy in Thailand is almost eighty years, slightly higher than the European and US averages and way above the rest of Southeast Asia, which is around seventy-three. The reason, explains *The Economist*, can be found in a surprisingly effective health system, considering that far less public money is spent than in more developed countries. In the 1970s fear of communist 'contagion' from neighbouring states encouraged successive governments to prioritise the development of rural areas, with health at the centre of ambitious infrastructure programmes, with the result that by 1990 all of Thailand's almost 1,000 districts had at least one hospital. The state also invested in education, training a generation of doctors and nurses who by law must spend the first three years of their careers in the villages. In 2002 Thaksin Shinawatra's government introduced a system of universal health coverage – the world's first in a middle-income nation – and, despite the subsequent political instability, successive governments have continued to expand this programme, which now also covers AIDS treatment and places a strong emphasis on prevention. In parallel, a private sector has developed that has made Thailand a destination for medical tourism. The rapidly ageing population will put the system to the test in years to come, but for now it works so well that other middle-income nations – from Southeast Asia to the Gulf – want to follow its lead and have asked for advice from the Thai government.

movements became a laughing stock in the official historical records: their insurgencies are collectively called the 'Rebellions of Crazies and Meritful Ghosts', a name that delegitimises their grievances by reducing them to mindlessly superstitious rebels. During the same period, in 1899, the term Isan was coined to replace Lao in the kingdom's administration to de-emphasise ethnic otherness and assimilate the population into Thai ethnicity. The Lao people in the region were subsequently moulded to become *khon Thai Isan*, 'Isan-Thai people'.

Regional interest in these historic rebellions has been flourishing in recent years, with independent initiatives to recover artefacts and uncover stories of the vanquished. (To remember, not replicate.) Also on the rise is an allergy to the term Isan. In the fervour for anti-absolutist revolution, for ethnic revindication or resistance to compulsory Thainess in general, Isan has become a politically incorrect term in certain circles; some avoid it altogether by pivoting to the five-syllable Thai word for northeast – *tawan-awk chiang nuea* – or by using common alternatives such as *thi-raap soong* (high plain) or by reverting to Lao in some fashion. Some refuse to extend the name of the region to its Lao dialects (the so-called *phasa Isan*, the Isan language) but are careful also not to mark the land as Lao, since the region's inhabitants include over a dozen Indigenous groups who not only pre-date the Lao but were also in some cases sold into slavery by them. Others invent new circumlocutions: a group of pro-democracy activists, for example, call themselves the People of Kong Chi Mun, referencing the three biggest rivers in the region.

In a way, this wave of proudly anti-Isan Isan regionalism is ironically reminiscent of an earlier variant of Isan regionalism that embraces the name. Proponents of the latter would argue that, while the word does mean northeast in Sanskrit, Isan doesn't necessarily imply subjugation to Bangkok: what about Emperor Isanavarman I and the empire of Isanapura, which ruled over these lands more than a thousand years ago? The empire left its mark with many monumental stone temples that stretch from the west to the east of Thailand and even into Laos and Cambodia!

Most Isan people belong to neither camp, however. While some are certainly happy to forget their ethnic background and assimilate into conservative Thainess, the rest of us are plenty proud of our heritage; it's just that we'd rather work – and play – with given labels and use them for our own purposes. Thainess ain't that absolute; there's no need for the regional chauvinism, which somehow tends to reek of male chauvinism as well, even when references are made to the 'matriarchy' or the 'sexual freedom' of traditional Lao society, the point of comparison always being the prudish and patriarchal Thai middle class – and that bar is not very high.

*

History and politics aside, the romantic attachment to Isan may also take apparently timeless and apolitical forms. Let's start, once again, with an outsider.

A day after the deadliest mass shooting and stabbing by a lone perpetrator in Thailand's history occurred at a daycare centre in a small Isan town on 6 October 2022, American travel writer David Luekens posted an article on his blog Thai Island Quest titled 'Violence Will Never Define Isaan'. Here's an excerpt:

> Anyone who has visited Isaan will have surely heard the rhythmic *plunk plunk plunk* of a wooden pestle tossing and bashing shards of green unripe papaya with lime juice, fermented fish sauce and fresh chili inside helmet-sized wooden mortars. At markets, street carts and front-stoop kitchens throughout the land, this unmistakable sound signals that the region's staple dish is about to be relished.
>
> Sharing *som tam* and other Isaan dishes appears to have been exactly what some of the first victims in Uthai Sawan were doing when they were killed.

Food is indeed central to Isan identity. The region famously has by far the hottest food in Thailand, and a lot of locals pride themselves on the level of heat they can handle, which can be measured by how many chilli peppers they'd like in their papaya salad.

But let's not forget that both chilli and papaya originated in Central America and that *som tam* came about in the intersection between maritime trade and forced migration in what is now Central Thailand and not the landlocked plateau. Back to the article:

> *Som tam* and its nourishing partner *khao niao* (sticky rice) are woven into the sense of peace that stirs inside me when visiting Isaan, or even daydreaming about it. Some part of me has been sadly dulled by the many mass shootings that have occurred in the US, and as an American, my reaction to the May massacre at a school in Uvalde, Texas, was more of anger and helplessness than sadness.
>
> But Isaan is not Texas (or Connecticut

or Colorado or ...). Although Thailand has a high gun-homicide rate, I truly did not believe that a mass killing of children would ever happen there – and especially not in a place like Uthai Sawan.

Above: Fishermen building a public platform for tourists on the banks of the Mekong in Loei province. It is becoming increasingly difficult to make a living from catching fish, so fishermen have to find other ways to make ends meet.
On page 96: A mother and daughter rolling in the mud – a traditional activity during the Bun Bang Fai festival when one's team rocket is set off.

The cognitive dissonance is palpable here. The author can't quite reconcile Isan's sensuous appeal and peaceful vibes with the uptick in senseless violence (this was not the only recent massacre in Isan). For me, what sticks out most is the contrast in the author's perception between the US Northeast and Northeast Thailand. His mentioning Connecticut in the same breath as Texas suggests that Connecticut, a 'deep blue' US state, has already been defined by violence in his mind because of the 2012 Sandy Hook Elementary School shooting, but he won't let the massacre at Uthai Sawan (a name which means Dawn of Paradise) take away his notion of Isan as a land of peace.

This hospitable image of Isan is happily reinforced by many Thais. Without discussing the NGO-ised ex-communists and the green urbanites who view provincial pastoral life to be antithetical to the big city's class stratification, individual alienation and environmental pollution, I'd like to point to the organic farmers under their patronage. Scattered throughout the country, they are a small minority of farmers who have managed to hold out against the onslaught of monoculture and chemical pesticides. Their sponsors include Red Bull and high-ranking government officials, and their rice is mainly exported to Europe.

I have visited one such model community several times as a chaperone and interpreter on a home-stay and study-abroad programme for US high-school students. There I had the best sticky rice of my life and also the most awkward speech I had to translate. In one exchange, a community elder lamented that more and more local youths were turning gay or trans because of the hormone-treated cow's milk in schools. I couldn't help but glance uneasily at a transgender student in the audience, who noticed I was cringing. I didn't translate it. I'm not sure who I was trying to protect: the one student, all the students, the farmer? And what was I protecting them from: discomfort, knowledge, accountability? Just as a fixation on resistance in political history tends to privilege male ways of negotiating with power, so those who obsess over the inviolability of traditional culture tend to misconstrue gender nonconformity and sexual diversity as pollution brought in from the outside.

Those in the diaspora aren't off the hook either. As we leave our homeland behind we can't help but carry with us a stuck-in-time version of it. We are now lucky enough not to have to keep up to date with the drug problems plaguing our younger people or suffer the floods that are a few weeks long instead of a few days because of the urbanisation of lowlands and swamps. Isan now represents life's simple pleasures, catching frogs in the muddy fields, grilling fish on a fragrant firewood stove, collecting red-ant eggs and mushrooms in the woods. A Facebook group called 'Picking

'Isan now represents life's simple pleasures, catching frogs in the muddy fields, grilling fish on a fragrant firewood stove, collecting red-ant eggs and mushrooms in the woods.'

Mushrooms Abroad' is a popular spot where this Isan is kept alive through mouth-watering close-ups of fungi supplied by hundreds of hobbyists, the majority of whom are Isan women in Europe. With over 95,000 members in the group, posts also involve other seasonal finds ('I was driving but had to stop to pick this wild garlic!'), safety checks ('Is this a wood ear mushroom?'), the law ('Today I learned Belgium strictly prohibits mushroom picking with a maximum fine of 50,000 euros! You girls in Sweden, Denmark, Finland, let's be friends!'), cautionary tales ('A grandma who visited her daughter's family in Europe just passed away from mushroom poisoning. This happens almost every year. Remember, folks, some that look the same as what we eat back home may be poisonous here!') and comedy ('After year ten my husband wasn't worried any more. He joins me in the woods now!'). A slice of rural Isan that's 100 per cent authentic but also happily removed from reality.

I have refrained from describing Isan as 'hybrid'. It's an idea I love to champion, but in order not to be reductive I'd have to put forward a case for the region as 'pure bred' as well. (For example, Lao dialects in Thailand are arguably more 'authentic' than those on the other side of the Mekong, as the former were spared the influences of French imperialism and insulated from changes imposed by the Laotian ruling classes.) With all these partial notions of Isan and its people – rebellious yet easy-going, forward-looking yet nostalgic, Thai yet un-Thai – it's best to look at it as if through a kaleidoscope. Becoming lost in the imaginary can be a good way to really get to know the place.

Dancing in the colourful lights of the nightly concerts during the Bun Bang Fai festival in Yasothon province.

The Bodiless Woman and Other Ghost Stories

Thailand is full of ghosts. Often, although not always, malevolent, they are suffering spirits as well as manifestations of a universal desire for life after death. Rather than asking whether they are real or not, it is wise to placate them with prayers and offerings.

Emma
Larkin

99

The first sighting took place around 2 a.m. in mid-September 2023 in a village in the Central Thai province of Lopburi.

A pig farmer known as Uncle Vichien was woken by his animals. His dogs were barking, the pigs were squealing and the ducks and chickens were squawking wildly. Uncle Vichien assumed a python had got into the pig shed and might be after the litter of piglets that had just been born. He grabbed a heavy shovel and went to investigate.

There was nothing untoward in the shed, but when Uncle Vichien walked around to the back of the building towards an area where the pigs' waste is channelled out to overgrown scrubland he came face to face with a terrifying vision: a *krasue*, one of Thailand's most feared ghosts.

As the creature was only a metre or two away, Uncle Vichien was in no doubt as to what he was looking at. It had all the characteristics of a *krasue*: a woman's head with no body, but dangling beneath its neck an exposed heart, lungs and intestines. It gave off an eerie red glow, and this particular one had the face of an old lady with short white hair. When it saw him, the *krasue* bared its teeth in a threatening manner. Uncle Vichien swung his shovel at the *krasue*, but it evaded his blow, soaring upwards and vanishing into the darkness.

EMMA LARKIN is the author of two non-fiction books about Myanmar, *Finding George Orwell in Burma* and *No Bad News for the King* (Penguin, USA), also published under the title *Everything is Broken* (Granta, UK). She is an American, born in the Philippines, raised in Thailand and educated in the United Kingdom. She has lived in Thailand for most of her life, and her latest book is the novel *Comrade Aeon's Field Guide to Bangkok* – which does, indeed, have some ghosts in it.

The next night, determined to catch the *krasue*, Uncle Vichien tied a dead duck to a tree; the *krasue* is said to feed on the carcasses of dead and rotting things. When the dogs started barking, he ran out to try to snare the *krasue*, but it was too fast for him and once again vanished into the night. Uncle Vichien later examined the duck and found that its carcass was intact but its entrails were missing. He surmised they must have been sucked out in their entirety by the hungry *krasue*.

The story spread quickly, and other people in the area came forward to say that they had seen something similar. Within days *krasue* sightings were being reported across five neighbouring districts. In a 'most urgent' report to the governor of Lopburi province, Uncle Vichien's local district chief described the atmosphere among local villagers as one of 'terror and panic'.

Such occurrences are not uncommon in Thailand, where a belief in ghosts is widespread and deeply ingrained. The pantheon of Thai ghosts is rich, varied, often gruesome and much feared. Ghost stories infuse popular culture, from literature and comics to soap operas, movies and TikTok videos, and almost everyone you meet has a ghost story to tell.

I grew up in Thailand, and perhaps as a result of having lived there most of my life I, too, am captivated by ghost stories. They were a (scary) part of my childhood and, later, an ever-present narrative undertone to life in Thailand. While most of my early writing was focused on neighbouring Burma/Myanmar, when I began writing a book about Thailand I knew it would be incomplete – even disingenuous – if there were no ghosts in it.

Most Thais are Buddhists – 93 per cent says the census data – but many also partake in the rituals and beliefs of other faiths absorbed from India and China via age-old trade routes and immigration. Hindu beliefs trickled down from the Brahmins who have, for centuries, overseen religious rites in the king's palace. Additionally, an animist streak pre-dates these spiritual borrowings and continues to underpin people's day-to-day actions. Protective amulets, often worn around the neck or waist, are a multimillion-dollar business. Elaborate blessings are routinely performed on new houses, cars and aeroplanes; before an aircraft is put into operation by the national carrier, Thai Airways, it is ceremonially blessed by monks. In the capital Bangkok, where driving can be dicey, taxis are often especially well protected with amulets and miniature shrines on their dashboards. My own car was blessed by a monk who inscribed an intricate yantra above the driver's seat and tied a holy tricoloured cloth around the steering column.

Spirits are also infused into the landscape and the very ground itself. Each plot of land is believed to have its own guardian spirit. Known as *jao thee* (literally, the lord of the land), these spirits can be benevolent and helpful or antagonistic and downright dangerous, depending on how well they are cared for by those living on or using the land. Almost every building in Thailand – no matter how big or small, historic or contemporary – has an accompanying spirit house in order to placate these potentially disruptive forces. On many plots there are two shrines: one for the *jao thee* and the other for more formalised guardian spirits. These miniature otherworldly dwelling places are installed at auspicious times and to specifications calculated by monks, Brahmins or fortune tellers. They range in style from simple shack-like structures in rural areas and wooden replicas of traditional Thai houses to tiny temple-like structures with gilded roofs or modern steel-and-glass complexes designed by professional architects for Bangkok's skyscrapers. A well-tended spirit house is propitiated daily with offerings of incense, candles, garlands of fresh flowers and any items favoured by the resident spirit – cigarettes or cheroots, whisky, soft drinks, cartons of milk, traditional Thai desserts served in banana-leaf bowls or, on special occasions, banquet-sized offerings of roast duck or pig.

In such a vibrant spiritual landscape, ghosts thrive.

*

While I was researching Thailand's haunted nature for my book, I came across a paper on Thai ghosts published in 1907 by a British surveyor called Arthur J. Irwin, who was a long-term employee of the Royal Survey Department of Siam, as the country was then known. Entitled 'Some Siamese Ghost-lore and Demonology', the

paper was first presented at the unlikely venue of the Engineering Society of Siam to an audience of specialists in medicine, law, history and religion.

During Irwin's travels across the country on surveying work, he fastidiously recorded details of local ghouls in a manner similar to an amateur naturalist compiling a field guide. More than a hundred years later the spectral landscape hasn't altered much. Modern-day guides, published in handy pocketbook formats, now include immigrant ghosts from Japan and Korea transported to Thailand via horror movies and subtitled soap operas – mostly zombie schoolgirls or long-haired women with bruised eyes who crawl out of air-conditioning vents – but Irwin's catalogue remains as good a primer as any on the ghosts that haunt Thailand today. The *krasue*, for instance, is covered by Irwin in some detail. Although Irwin notes that some of its attributes 'vary considerably' according to his different interlocutors, there existed certain consistencies that continue to this day. The *krasue* is believed to be associated with a living human being who appears normal by day but by night becomes possessed by the *krasue* and leaves their corporeal body to go out and hunt down food that Irwin refers to as the 'dirtiest matters'. Although he was likely too proper to list the *krasue*'s specific taste for raw or rotting flesh and faeces, he drolly observes that she makes for a 'most unpleasant neighbour'.

Irwin's catalogue covers even more fantastical ghosts that are still part of the common lexicon. There is the gigantic and pitiful *phi pret*, which can vary in height from ten to sixteen metres: 'Its mouth is exceedingly small, even as the eye of a needle, so that it can never satisfy its hunger.' The *phi krahang* has the appearance of a man but 'with feathers and a tail like a bird', and which today is generally believed to be the spirit of a person who has dabbled in black magic and been overtaken by the dark arts.

One frequently encountered ghost is invisible but persistent. Known as the *phi am*, it squats on a person's chest and renders them temporarily paralysed. You will know you are the victim of a *phi am* if, in those uncertain moments between sleep and wakefulness, you find yourself struggling for breath and unable to move your limbs.

Irwin notes that the experience 'reminds one of what is spoken of in English as a nightmare'.

By far the most feared ghost of all is the *phi tai hong*, or the spirit of someone who has died a violent death. In Irwin's time such sudden endings were 'caused by weapons, by falling from a tree or building, or in child birth'. Today, car accidents, plane crashes and political conflict can be added to that list. Irwin describes the *phi tai hong* as 'distinctly malevolent'.

In Bangkok, the eccentric landlady of a house I rented for many years lived nearby in the same compound. It was rumoured in the neighbourhood that, years earlier, our landlady had murdered her in-laws. One neighbour even claimed to have seen the aftermath, telling me, 'She bludgeoned them to death – there was blood everywhere!' The rumours had it that she escaped justice because her family was wealthy and able to bribe the police. But a different kind of justice was suggested in the stories that persisted about the *phi tai hong* that haunted the house in which the murder had taken place – a suitably spooky old wooden building next to the landlady's home. People sometimes heard a piano being played inside the house, although it had been rented out (to an unwitting foreigner) and no longer had a piano. Every so often an old man was seen gazing out from under the filigreed eaves of the upstairs window. So when our landlady had an accident at home and broke both her legs in a fall down the stairs, no one in the neighbourhood was in any doubt as to what had happened. She herself told me she felt like she'd been pushed but couldn't say by whom or what. The neighbour who witnessed the bloody aftermath of the murder only shook her head knowingly at me and warned, 'You must always remember that a *phi tai hong* is the most dangerous kind of ghost.'

*

'Ghosts will manifest wherever something really terrible has happened to someone,' explains Kapol Thongplub, or Pong, as Thailand's most famous ghost hunter is known. 'People see them in old temples or abandoned houses, but they're also found in modern buildings like hotels and condominiums. Basically, all you need for

a ghost story to flourish in a certain place is for someone to have died there.'

Pong has been obsessed with ghosts since he was a young boy, and there is little he doesn't know about the Thai spirit pantheon. He made his name through a late-night radio show called *The Shock*, which features audio recordings of him and his ghost-hunting team investigating hauntings around the country and also has a segment for people to phone in and talk about their encounters with ghosts. *The Shock* was launched in the early 1990s, and its sustained popularity is an indicator of just how haunted Thailand is: the show is broadcast daily Monday to Friday for three hours a day and has yet to run out of new material.

I arranged to meet Pong as part of my research into Thai ghosts when I heard that his team kept an archive of all these tales, including photographs, video clips, letters and audio recordings. We meet at his office, which is piled high with stacks of printed-out sheets detailing all the prospective ghost stories listeners send in. From the blood-stained streets around the Democracy Monument, where anti-government demonstrators have been shot dead by soldiers over past decades, to lonely stretches of country road where fatal car accidents have taken place, this unique database charts the night terrors and morbid weak spots of an entire nation. Pong refers to it as a 'ghost encyclopaedia'.

The encyclopaedia likely contains the descriptions and actions of every type of ghost ever seen in Thailand. There are reports of 19th-century royal concubines, glinting with gold from their earrings, bracelets and anklets, as well as peasant farmers who move through the gloom clad only in *pha khao maa*, the roughly woven cotton cloth used as a sarong in the countryside. There are headless ghosts ('bodies without heads, heads without bodies') and the ghosts of corpses that have been chopped into pieces and disposed of in toilets, rivers or city canals. There are plenty of what Pong calls Thailand's 'signature ghosts' – the same ones charted by the British surveyor Irwin more than a century ago, such as the *phi pret*. And there are also *farang*, or Western, ghosts – 'So many of you visit this country, after all, the odds are some of you are going to die here,' says Pong.

Horror is not a prerequisite for every ghost story, and Thailand's most famous ghost – 'our national ghost', as Pong puts it – resides within what is essentially a love story. Nang Nak ('Lady' Nak) was a villager who lived in a traditional Thai wooden house on stilts in the village of Phra Khanong – an area that has today been subsumed by Bangkok's urban sprawl – some time in the 19th century. She was pregnant when her husband left the village to fight in a war against a neighbouring country, and both she and her baby died when she was giving birth. When her husband returned home after the war he was greeted by her lifelike ghost and settled back into their house not realising his wife and child were dead. Nak continued about her daily chores, singing lullabies to her ghostly baby and cooking meals for her husband. It wasn't until a lime fell between the floorboards and Nak reached out with a supernaturally elongated arm to pick it up from the ground below that her husband realised she was no longer alive. Her vision of a happy family shattered, Nak turned murderous and killed villagers who tried to convince her husband to leave his haunted house.

The story of Nang Nak straddles an amorphous line between fact and fantasy. In what is today Phra Khanong district in Bangkok you can visit the temple where Nak's spirit is said to reside. The shrine is famous for providing winning lottery numbers, but, given Nak's own tragic circumstances, it is also believed to help those trying to avoid military conscription. In a glass cabinet within the temple compound lies a preserved foetus – allegedly that of Nak's stillborn baby – which devotees propitiate with offerings of milk, sweets and toys.

Whether or not the tale of Nang Nak has any foundation in fact, the themes of loss and yearning clearly resonate with the Thai psyche, and her story is constantly told and retold, in books and comics as well as in soap operas, movies and even musicals.

In Thai Buddhist cosmology there are thirty-one planes of existence divided into three worlds: the world of desire (eleven realms), the world of celestial being (sixteen realms) and the highest world without material substance (four realms). The realm of humans exists in the lower half of the world of desire. It sits just above the lowest realms of loss and woe, which contain the respective realms of animals, suffering ghosts, demons and then the descending hells, each one successively more grizzly than the one above it. A person's karmic store of good and bad deeds committed throughout life determines which of these three worlds their spirit will be reborn into, at what level and for how long.

The classic text on this cosmology – the 14th-century *Trai Phum Phra Ruang*, or *Three Worlds According to King Ruang: A Thai Buddhist Cosmology* (translated by Frank E. Reynolds and Mani B. Reynolds) – states: 'What accompanies one [after death] is only merit and evil; they will produce results and become [a] being. As a result of this evil and merit, the being will be fortunate or unfortunate – some are beautiful and some are not beautiful; some have a long life, and some have a short life; some are lords over others, and some are the slaves of others; some enjoy good conditions, and some are unfortunate; some have understanding, and some have no understanding.'

According to the *Trai Phum*, ghosts inhabit the realm between animals and demons; they have not yet acquired enough merit to be reborn as an animal nor enough demerit to become a demon or be cast into one of the progressively worsening levels of hell. For this reason, the first thing many Thais do after seeing a ghost is to make merit – through prayer and offerings – for the suffering spirit. Ghost hunter Pong adheres to this practice on a daily basis and makes merit, as he describes it, 'for the world of things unseen and for beings less fortunate than we humans'. As Pong sees it, the travails of human life are mirrored in stories from other realms of existence. 'As long as we exist in a cycle of birth, pain, ageing and death we will continue to see ghosts,' he says with conviction. 'It's basic human nature to want our stories to continue. It's not just a Thai thing – it's universal – although I will concede that, as a nation, we Thais are especially good at seeing ghosts.'

*

In the case of the *krasue* spotted by the pig farmer Uncle Vichien, events reached a peak when a local resort owner offered a one-million-baht reward for anyone who could capture the *krasue*. Ghost hunters hoping to win the prize descended on the neighbourhood and drove through the night on motorbikes, further exacerbating the heightened emotions of local villagers. And they didn't come unarmed: in a TikTok video one ghost hunter showed off his special ghost-hunting sword, blessed by a famous monk.

The district chief held a press conference to announce a rational explanation for what Uncle Vichien had seen. The official story was that a discarded mask had been found near Uncle Vichien's farm, proving that what he had seen was not a *krasue* but a chicken thief attempting to steal his flock. Uncle Vichien scoffed when he saw the Halloween-style mask presented by the district office as evidence. 'Tell me,' he reasoned in an interview with the press, 'can a human being float? What I saw was floating above the ground, and I promise you it was *not* human.'

The national media picked up on the story, and all the major channels and newspapers covered the Lopburi *krasue* scare. Various experts spoke out to disprove the existence of the *krasue*, including one forensic doctor who patiently explained that the anatomy of the *krasue* was implausible. 'It's just not possible to have organs existing without the supporting mechanism of a skeleton, blood vessels and musculature – the human body works as a whole,' he said, clearly not having heard, or not understanding, Uncle Vichien's statement that what he had seen was most definitely *not* human.

Both the police and the local administrative authorities took to going door to door across the district and patrolling at night to try to assuage people's fears. The authorities in Lopburi also requested that the resort owner rescind his reward to deter any further ghost hunters and urged Uncle Vichien and other witnesses to refrain from speaking to the press. The story eventually died down, and presumably life went back to normal in Lopburi, but I can't help thinking that Uncle Vichien won the battle of narratives that had taken place.

To my mind there's really no contest between the story of a chicken thief wearing a Halloween mask and a floating female head with innards that glow in the dark. If some ghosts, like the *phi tai hong*, promise the possibility of posthumous justice in cases where there is none in life and other ghosts are the manifestations of a person's

misdeeds committed in a previous incarnation, they play a role as societal checking mechanisms – visceral reminders of morality and mortality. As such, Uncle Vichien's *krasue* conjures up a force ancient and uncontrollable, something that is other than what we are and more than what we know. The po-faced experts and administrative authorities insisting on prosaic, science-based explanations hardly stood a chance.

Ultimately, preaching veracity in such contexts may be missing the point. Pong told me that when he and his team sift through the hundreds of ghost stories they receive each day they aren't fact checking or analysing details; rather, they're looking for a good story. 'I'm not going to come down on one side or the other as to whether these sightings are true, false or somewhere in between,' says Pong. 'But I will stand by the undeniable fact that they provide rollicking good stories, and, for me, that's what counts the most.'

A Concise Encyclopaedia of Thai Ghosts

Phi Kee

MEANING: 'Shit ghost', roughly speaking
ORIGIN: Lao folklore
WHERE THEY ARE FOUND: In the toilet, usually after a nightmare.
WHAT TO DO IF YOU MEET ONE: Before flushing the toilet, it is considered good manners to ask the ghost politely to let your excrement flush away in peace, removing any misfortune that might accompany it

CHARISMA/STAR POWER: ★★
Perhaps not as glamourous as other ghosts, but probably the most useful – especially for fans of street food
FEAR FACTOR: ★
Pretty cute, so almost impossible to resist the temptation to take one back home in your suitcase

Nang Nak

WHO SHE WAS: Nak was a beautiful woman who died in childbirth while her husband was on military service
SUPERPOWER: Can make her arms stretch like the *Street Fighter* character Dhalsim
WHO SHE PROTECTS: Pregnant women and men who want to avoid conscription
WHAT TO DO TO WIN HER FAVOUR: A visit to her temple in Bangkok's Phra Khanong neighbourhood with offerings of fruit, lotus and incense

CHARISMA/STAR POWER: ★★★★★
The undisputed star of the pantheon, featured in countless films, TV series, books, comic strips and cartoons
FEAR FACTOR: ★★
After all, not even her husband noticed that she was a ghost after he came back from the army – but she can turn nasty if anyone tries to persuade her husband of the truth

Phi Nang Lum

CLASSIFICATION: Belongs to the infamous category of *phi tai hong*, the ghosts of those who died a violent death, who are among the most feared
WHO SHE WAS: A traditional dancer killed out of jealousy (either by a lover or a rival, depending on which version of the story you hear)
SUPERPOWER: When she appears, in traditional dress with blood running down her face and sometimes oozing from severed body parts, she performs a terrifying dance to the sound of pounding drums

CHARISMA/STAR POWER: ★★★★
She appears in many horror films, and the traditional music accompanying her macabre dance also makes her a sort of ambassador for Thai culture
FEAR FACTOR: ★★★★★
Like all *phi tai hong*, she is difficult to exorcise and tends to haunt homes

Nang Tani

APPEARANCE: A beautiful woman, often portrayed in green traditional clothing, with greenish skin, long black hair and scarlet lips; she only appears on full-moon nights and hovers a few centimetres above the ground
HABITAT: She is the spirit of the wild banana tree (*tani* in Thai), which is where she makes her home; there are many tree spirits in Thailand, known collectively as *nang mai*
HOW TO WIN HER FAVOUR: The most important rule goes without saying: don't cut down the banana tree she lives in; you can also offer her sweets, incense or flowers and tie a coloured ribbon around the tree trunk

CHARISMA/STAR POWER: ★★★★
She is very popular and stars in a classic of Thai cinema, *Nang Phrai Tani* (1967), as well as many comic strips, in which she often plays a comedy role
FEAR FACTOR: ★★
She tends to be benevolent – sometimes even feeding passing monks – but she can also mete out fatal punishment to men who have treated women badly

Krasue

APPEARANCE: A woman's disembodied head with her entrails still attached; by day she lives among us as an ordinary person
DISTRIBUTION AND HABITAT: With local twists, she is present right across Southeast Asia
HOW TO PROTECT YOURSELF: At night the headless body is vulnerable, as it can be hidden or dismembered, and if the head does not find its body again by morning it dies
A PRACTICAL TIP: After her gory meals she has a habit of wiping her mouth on clothes hung out to dry, so it is best to do your laundry in the morning

CHARISMA/STAR POWER: ★★★★
The Cambodian version, known as an *arb*, starred in the first film made in the country after the fall of the Khmer Rouge, the 1980 horror film *My Mother Is an Arb*
FEAR FACTOR: ★★★★★
Her diet, in order of preference, consists of human flesh, blood, animal carcasses and faeces (human or animal) – so even her eating habits are terrifying!

Phi Pret

WHO THEY ARE: Tall and very thin, like a coconut palm, they are the ghosts of those who were materialistic and ungrateful to their parents in life and have been reincarnated as hungry beings unable to sate their appetite and thirst through their tiny mouths
PROVENANCE: They are closely related to the *preta*, or hungry ghosts, of the Buddhist tradition
WHERE TO FIND THEM: Around temples and religious festivals, trying to convince the living to make offerings and say prayers to make merit for them

CHARISMA/STAR POWER: ★★★
They are quite awkward, with their giant hands and shambling gait, but often immortalised as large statues, for example in the Hell Garden at the Wat Muang temple north of Ayutthaya
FEAR FACTOR: ★★
With their unending quest for forgiveness and redemption, they inspire more pity than fear, even though they can be bad tempered and aggressive

Farang Ghosts

CLASSIFICATION: The ghosts of Westerners (*farang*) who have died in Thailand
DISTRIBUTION AND HABITAT: They are rare, but there was a spike in sightings after the 2004 tsunami, especially on the islands of Phuket and Phi Phi
THE MAIN EXPLANATIONS OF THEIR RELATIVE SCARCITY ON REDDIT:
1) Ghosts of dead *farang* go back to haunt their native countries; 2) *Farang* have no soul, so when they die there is nothing left

CHARISMA/STAR POWER: ★
Even alive, the average Western tourist is nothing special
FEAR FACTOR: ★
Frankly, not high

Other ghosts tourists should keep an eye out for

PHI LANG KLUANG: Around a beach bonfire in the south, you are approached by a stranger who appears normal until he asks you to scratch his back, at which point you will see an open wound right through his body infested with maggots and millipedes

PHI PHONG: Smells terrible and feeds mainly on frogs – not particularly dangerous to humans, but it is better to keep your distance if you hear croaking, as the ghost will attack if threatened, and if you accidentally swallow its saliva you will also become a *phi phong*

PHI KONG KOI: Hops on its single leg repeating the word 'koi, koi, koi' (hence the name) through a sort of proboscis; lives in the forests and is a nuisance because of its habit of sucking blood from the toes of sleeping campers; to protect yourself, keep your feet together or your ankles crossed

A Concise Encyclopaedia of Thai Ghosts

Add a Pinch of Coriander

Taking its cue from Japan and South Korea – and conscious of Thailand's untapped potential – the Thai establishment is focusing on soft power to boost the nation's prestige and its economy. Often, however, its measures are timid and fail to go far enough to stimulate a debate and bolster a cultural ecosystem in which freedom of thought and speech are still on shaky ground.

VALERIA PALERMI
Translated by Eleanor Chapman

The Museum of Contemporary Art (MOCA) in Bangkok displays its permanent collection as well as temporary exhibitions of work by great Thai artists.

It didn't go down well in Bangkok, but the Singaporeans knew what they were doing when they offered Taylor Swift a contract worth around $17 million for exclusivity on her shows in Southeast Asia. In March 2024 six dates of the Eras Tour were held in the Lion City, leaving the other ASEAN countries with nothing. From Manila to Bangkok, Swifties flew to Singapore bringing with them vast sums of money. Between $259 million and $369 million were spent on hotels, food and entertainment, according to Chua Hak Bin, an economist at Maybank.

Thailand's prime minister at the time, Srettha Thavisin, expressed public outrage. But on *Thai Enquirer* – a news, politics and culture website – analyst Wanchai Vatanakool urged the government to 'use Taylor Swift disappointment to fuel Thai soft power' – let's dazzle the world with our *own* talent and creativity. Let's be like Japan and South Korea with cinema, music and art. We can become a 'powerhouse of cultural exports', too; we've got the talent and the resources.

Really?

Soft power is spoken about a lot in Thailand, but not always in the way the expression was coined by American political scientist Joseph S. Nye Jr in reference to the ability to influence others not through force or coercion but appeal and attraction, through culture, values (such as democracy and human rights) and foreign policy. The previous administration – that of Prayut Chan-o-cha – had already announced that they would seduce the world and make a fortune through focusing on the 'Five Fs' (food, film, fashion, fighting and festivals), but the ambition grew with Srettha Thavisin's government. Now there are eleven branches of the Thai soft power industry: art, food, design, publishing, festivals and events, film, theatre and TV, gaming and esports, fashion, music, sport and tourism.

The National Soft Power Strategy Committee was established, divided into eleven subcommittees. In the beginning it was run by Thavisin and by Paetongtarn Shinawatra, known familiarly as Ung Ing – daughter of the perennial revenant of Thai politics Thaksin Shinawatra – who has now become Thailand's prime minister. Its purpose: to make Thailand more competitive on the global market by accelerating its cultural economy. Its plan: to generate over a period of not less than four years a minimum annual income

VALERIA PALERMI is an Italian journalist who, before moving to Thailand, was a correspondent for *la Repubblica*, director of *la Repubblica*'s weekly supplement *D* and editor-in-chief of *L'Espresso* and *Marie Claire*. Among her interests are fashion, culture and travel. When she's not in Bangkok she can be found in Marseille, convinced that cities of dubious reputation can be surprising hubs of opportunity. She currently works with a number of Italian newspapers and weeklies.

of four trillion baht (approximately $115 billion) and to create twenty million new jobs through the OFOS (One Family One Soft Power) initiative that aims to foster talent in every Thai family. Its hope: to follow in the footsteps of South Korea – whose Korean Wave (*Hallyu*) has seduced East and West with everything from pop to beauty and fashion, TV and cinema to literature – or Cool Japan, a government-led initiative which, for decades, has been behind the export of cars and motorbikes, manga and anime, fashion and technology. And so Thailand's response to the Korea Creative Content Agency (KOCCA) is the Thailand Creative Content Agency (THACCA).

Following this lead, Silpakorn University launched an undergraduate programme in music and the entertainment business, with the goal of feeding young people into the entertainment industry. It offers courses in, to name a few, singing, dancing and social media marketing. It is perhaps thanks to this energy that Thailand is rising in the Global Soft Power Index carried out every year by the consultancy Brand Finance.

But is stringing together eleven branches of soft power enough to generate rivers of money? Or do you need a strong cultural context, an ecosystem of big museums hosting big exhibitions, globally competitive brands, a reservoir of talent and creative industries making products that the world does actually want to 'buy'? This is the question bouncing around Bangkok's cultural communities, alongside hushed criticism of a lack of serious strategy. Too many ingredients have been added to the melting pot of 'Thai soft power' in the hope that the broth will turn out tasty: from mango and sticky rice (the rapper Milli caused a sensation at Coachella Festival in 2022 when she ate the national dessert on stage) to the (ugly) elephant pants that used to be worn only by tourists but have become a cool trend among young Thais. Soft power is Lisa, the only Thai member of the Korean girl band Blackpink; the band has more than a hundred million followers on Instagram. Soft power with more testosterone is Muay Thai; at the forty-third Cobra Gold annual Thai–US military exercises, the Thai government asked Thai-boxing legend Buakaw Banchamek to train the US soldiers in the art of Muay Thai, while in the second half of 2024 another eight experts went to Saudi Arabia to train local soldiers and professional boxers. Soft power is Anntonia Porsild, the Thai beauty queen who was runner-up in Miss Universe 2023.

But, despite all this excitement, not everything in the government's strategy is going entirely to plan. A survey conducted in late 2023 revealed that few people really knew what the OFOS strategy was, and the announcement of the Thailand Creative Content Agency had been confusing, given that there already was a Creative Economy Agency. In February 2024 there were mass resignations from the entire fashion subcommittee of the National Soft Power Strategy Committee, which subsequently came to be chaired by Achara Umpujh, vice-president of the Mall Group, whose portfolio boasts several of the most spectacular shopping complexes in Bangkok: Siam Paragon, EmQuartier and Emporium. Meanwhile, then-Prime Minister Srettha Thavisin announced that the committee would have to cut back its 5.1 million baht (*c*. $150,000) budget.

*

NOT-SO-SOFT POWER

No one is a prophet in their own land, and so it was that an Estonian businessman had the idea for Prison Fight – a programme that organises Muay Thai contests in which Thai prisoners fight foreign opponents in order to punch their way to a reduction in their sentences. The idea has inspired documentaries, films and TV series that provide a platform for the Thai martial art, even though Kirill Sokur didn't actually come up with anything new. The Thai prison system has a long history of sporting competitions aimed at incentivising a healthy lifestyle for prisoners, and occasionally, if their performances were a 'source of pride' for the nation, they would be granted a pardon. Amnat Ruenroeng was serving fifteen years for theft, but thanks to his victories in boxing matches in prison he was granted a pardon that saw him compete in the 2008 Olympics just a year after his release. The tradition of earning your freedom in this way has a long history, and it is said that as early as 1774 the legendary boxer Nai Khanom Tom, jailed after Ayutthaya ended up in Burmese hands, was invited to challenge the best Burmese fighters. After he had defeated them all the Burmese king paid tribute to his prowess by setting him free. Today Muay Thai exploits are chiefly drivers of tourism and soft power, which the government takes very seriously (in 2012 it even banned the competing discipline of MMA), granting a special ninety-day visa for those who visit Thailand to learn the secrets of the martial art.

'What does soft power really mean? The government uses it as a catch-all. I get the idea: we want to be like South Korea,' says Kong Rithdee, film critic and director. 'In just a few decades they were able to become the biggest or second-biggest cultural exporters in the world. Everyone's talking about K-pop, K-beauty, K-drama. But that was possible because they know how to speak to the world, mixing comedy and high drama. Look at *Parasite*. It deals with inequality in such an unflinching way, in a language that everyone can understand. Korea played the long game with soft power and got both public and private sectors involved. There was clear thinking behind it. They got rid of censorship and nurtured talent.'

Thailand has enormous potential, but it has work to do. 'They're trying. They're reducing censorship, for example. But they want quick results – that's how politicians are – and that won't work. You want Thai cinema to be successful internationally? It'll take at least ten, fifteen years. There's already so much produced here, from Thailand and abroad, but there needs to be support for new generations. You can't measure success only in economic terms – how many films you sell internationally, how much you make from your artists and locations. Nurturing a cultured, stimulated general public makes a difference. If you create skills, you strengthen the entire ecosystem of cultural industries.'

The 2023 film *Hunger* was very successful, Rithdee explains, but a lot of that is due to it being on Netflix, and anyway it was an isolated case. 'There's a need to nurture the talented Thai artists who are producing quality work. We've already got Nawapol Thamrongrattanarit, Banjong Pisanthanakun,

A Bearbrick yak statue in front of a hotel in Bangkok. Yaks, or giants – which feature in many artworks – are figures from Buddhist tradition; they act as guardians to protect against spiritual enemies.

Add a Pinch of Coriander

Kongdej Jaturanrasamee – they're famous even with young, international audiences. We've got the Boys' Love series – now that is Thai soft power. They're popular in other Asian countries and in South America, perhaps because *telenovelas* are similar to Thai soap operas. We need to seem like a country that is open to people and new ideas. It's time to build the Thailand brand.'

Something that will undoubtedly contribute to this, and one that the Tourism Authority of Thailand has enthusiastically encouraged, is the filming of the third season of *The White Lotus,* an HBO series that has already benefited from Hawaiian and Sicilian locations. In February 2024 they started shooting in Bangkok, Phuket and Koh Samui. The cast includes both the veteran actress Patravadi 'Lek' Mejudhon and the venerated Lisa. In 2023 the Thai government approved a plan to make it even easier for foreign productions to be produced in Thailand, and, as part of an incentive scheme, the foreign cast – including Leslie Bibb, Jason Isaacs, Michelle Monaghan, Parker Posey and Natasha Rothwell – will not have to pay Thai taxes.

Chalida Uabumrungjit – director of the Thai Film Archive, member of the National Soft Power Strategy Committee and a key figure in Thai cultural circles – has raised some concerns. 'We have an important film industry,' she explains.

Opposite top: A crew from Jungka Studio, one of Thailand's leading production houses, prepares to film an action scene. In recent years the Thai film industry has grown steadily, reaching audiences in many countries and winning international awards.
Opposite bottom: A Muay Thai fight at the stadium in Chiang Mai.

'We're a hub for both Thai and foreign productions. Foreign productions can benefit from rebates of 15 to 20 per cent, but the people who work on them aren't working for Thailand. Netflix has been making films here for a while, but they're considered foreign productions because it's Netflix who's paying for them. Thai governments have always looked at how much money they can make from foreign productions rather than Thai cinema. But now they're starting to understand that there's a problem with intellectual property and authors' rights. If a film produced in Thailand gets screened all over the world, the rights belong to the foreign production company, not to us,' she argues. 'We're a minority in our own country – we don't get subsidies or tax breaks; we work for others. Of course, as an individual you can make good money, but the film industry as a whole can't. There needs to be more funding for Thai productions, more support for homegrown talent, otherwise they'll leave the country and find success abroad. They don't stand a chance here.'

Film and TV come under the same soft power subcommittee led by Chalermchatri Yukol (Adam), Chalida continues. The plan is that THACCA will be established within the next two years, 'meanwhile there are ongoing discussions about OFOS, which is supposed to train twenty million people and generate a basic income of more than 200,000 baht ($6,000) per year per family. Upskilling people on low incomes will uplift the entire economy. Our films will be at all the festivals: Berlin, Osaka, Hong Kong, Cannes. The committee will support both commercial and independent cinema, and there will be extra budget for Boys' Love series.

We want to promote Thai cinema and provide training. As for learning from Korea? I've been watching them for twenty-five years. The industry there makes demands, it fights to make things happen, it doesn't wait for things to fall from the sky. We're looking to Korea, Taiwan, Singapore. We're trying to learn from everyone quickly.'

Learning and education are one of Thailand's key issues. The results from the last PISA report (the OECD's Programme for International Student Assessment) were worse than ever, revealing deep flaws in the Thai education system. 'It doesn't foster skills or creativity. We make our students rote-learn everything, and that doesn't encourage critical thinking, whether in history or in other subjects. It's an authoritarian model,' comments Narisa Chakrabongse, writer and founder of River Books Publishing. 'Attention to soft power is welcome, so long as it's not superficial. There's a Thai saying, "Add a pinch of coriander on top", the idea being, whatever the dish, if you add coriander it will be delicious. A trick, basically. My hope is that this doesn't all turn out to be a gimmick. The last time I was at the Frankfurt Book Fair I didn't see a Thai stand. Our publishing industry is struggling; we're up against powerful foreign groups. We've got to promote our culture abroad. Our embassies should be telling the world that Thailand has more to offer than delicious food, spectacular beaches and beautiful women. Art, for example – just think of the biennales in Bangkok or Chiang Rai.'

'I went to that one and really liked it – especially in Chiang Saen, along the Mekong River,' intervenes Pinaree Sanpitak, a Thai artist who is famous the world over, in particular for her work reflecting on the feminine form, including her 'Breast Stupas'. 'The pieces were spread throughout the city, in temples, schools and parks. All the curators were Thai; they did a great job organising a biennale on the themes of migration, the environment and politics. They brought in both international artists and interesting Thai artists such as Nipan Oranniwesna, Tawatchai Puntusawasdi, Busui Ajaw and the Baan Noorg initiative. You have to be so determined to make it as an artist today. On paper young people have more opportunities than ever before, but in my opinion they moan too much, they're posting and messaging online too much. If they did less of that, they'd get more done. It's not easy being an artist. You need patience, time and hard work if you want to make your mark.'

*

Fashion – one of the Five Fs from the first soft power strategy – is also still playing an important role. In March 2024 Prime Minister Srettha Thavisin met Pascal Morand, executive president of the Fédération de la Haute Couture et de la Mode, the governing body of the French fashion industry, to discuss the possibility of making Thailand a Southeast Asian centre of fashion and design. But can Thai fashion stand out on an international level?

'Our fashion industry is not strong, it's a bit all over the place, a bit thrown together. There have been attempts to support the sector, even by setting up governmental agencies, but they always seem to focus on minor things. Our fashion weeks are nothing like in Milan or Paris. I don't take part in them; I prefer to go it alone,' says Shone Puipia, one of Bangkok's strongest young designers. Son of the artists Pinaree Sanpitak and

GASTRODIPLOMACY

'The way to a man's heart is through his stomach' must have been the Thai government's thinking when it launched its Global Thai programme – the idea being to broaden its influence around the world through food. The strategy, which began in 2002 and has been much imitated – including by South Korea, well known for its own work on soft power – included the publication by the Health Ministry of a *Manual for Thai Chefs Going Abroad*, which provides information on everything from recruitment and staff training to foreign tastes. But the most significant part of this 'gastrodiplomacy' operation – a term coined by *The Economist* to describe Global Thai – was the creation of various forms of incentive: those who open a Thai restaurant abroad have access to subsidised loans, commercial assistance, market analysis and, in certain cases – such as those going to New Zealand – special visas. A year into the programme the number of Thai restaurants around the world had grown from 5,500 to 8,000 and by 2018 there were 15,000, and once the restaurants were open the government was at pains to guarantee their quality, creating the Thai Select certificate, a sort of seal of approval for authentic restaurants, from fast-food outlets to haute cuisine. The results of this 'edible branding' exercise, which is part of the larger plan to expand Thai soft power, are tangible, with the country duly achieving record numbers of foreign visitors.

Chatchai Puipia, he trained at the Royal Academy of Fine Arts in Antwerp.

'A lot of the soft power initiatives talk about promoting traditional dress, but in my opinion it's a bit much to ask contemporary Thai labels to put out special collections with silk or traditional fabrics and patterns. It's not easy to make that work – no one wants to wear things from a bygone era. Also, perhaps, traditional dress is associated with the monarchy, with ceremony; it belongs to a world that feels distant and unappealing to many people. Thai society has eclectic tastes in fashion. Our fashion is a bit quirky, eccentric; it never takes itself too seriously. That's a blessing and a curse at the same time,' Puipia says, citing several other interesting designers, including Vvon Sugunnasil, Vinn Patararin, the IWANNABANGKOK collective and Philip Huang. 'We want to dismantle the sense of appropriateness that there is in Western fashion. Our high-end products are looser, more casual, because they've adapted to a tropical environment. You can't make structured garments here like you might in Milan. Along with carefully picked-out fabrics, prints and colours, there is an irony in my designs. In general, clothes are less gendered here, and there is more fluidity than there is in the West. When I'm designing, I don't necessarily have either a male or a female body in mind.'

His suggestions for the soft power committee? 'A showcase of Thai designers in Paris or London. Brainstorming sessions for Thai creatives to come up with ideas for how we can put ourselves on the global stage. They should listen to us; we designers have interesting things to say. These pieces of cloth say a lot about our freedom, too.'

An interesting way of rethinking

'How much soft power can be wielded by a country that still uses such a heavy hand?'

tradition while also looking to the contemporary comes from Doi Tung, a long-standing social enterprise in the centre of the Golden Triangle, the famous opium-producing region spanning northern Thailand, Myanmar and Laos. The organisation has several branches (community impact, handicrafts, tourism and the production of coffee and macadamia) including fashion.

Diskul Dispanadda (Duke), CEO of the Doi Tung Development Project, explains. 'Sustainability is one of the most powerful trends in fashion, and we also want our clothes to be sustainable rather than aiming for bold, cool designs. That's the idea behind our Everyday Collection: accessible fashion for every day, clothes that can be worn on multiple occasions. It is local craftspeople who make the fabric and turn it into clothes. We use simple patterns and plain colours so we're not mixing too many fabrics. That way we get through a lot of fabric a day and can keep our prices low. We're trying to diversify the colours.'

Sustainability at Doi Tung, Duke continues, is also a question of long-term employment for local communities, the selection of raw materials, the use of recycled materials, including thread made from plastic bottles. 'We're thinking of using fewer and fewer models. If we want a collection for everyone, we should design it based on our staff, on normal people. The strategy is to lower prices and be more accessible. Fashion without a conscience won't get you anywhere. If we keep on exploiting natural resources, there won't be anything left for the next generation.'

When it comes to soft power, Duke thinks that Thailand is at a point in which 'we need to redefine ourselves. Thai cinema can be used for soft power; music probably can't. Sport is getting there; Muay Thai is global now. Maybe in the future medical tourism could become a soft power – our healthcare is very advanced.'

*

There is an elephant in the room, however, one that the Thai government is cautiously sidestepping. But it's an important question: how much soft power can be wielded by a country that still uses such a heavy hand, where there are critical political problems, where democratically elected governments are deposed by coups and the constitution is changed according to the whims of a military-backed government? A country where democracy is still conditional and limited. One where, as Mark S. Cogan, associate professor of peace and conflict studies at Kansai Gaidai University in Osaka, has written: 'soft power is easily negated by the use of hard power'. Cogan was writing in the *Bangkok Post* in January 2024, the month in which the harshest ever sentence for a *lèse-majesté* conviction was imposed on an activist in their thirties for publications deemed defamatory.

The road ahead for the soft power committee is long but hopeful. A Thai journalist who wanted to remain anonymous reflected, 'it's Thaksin Shinawatra and his team behind it – after all, his daughter is the vice-president [now prime minister], isn't she? I don't like him [Thaksin Shinawatra] very much,

Above: Nana Coffee Roasters in Ari, one of Bangkok's most popular neighbourhoods; high-quality coffee beans are grown widely in Northern Thailand.
Below: The creations of Thai fashion designer Shone Pupia offer a unique and uncompromising take on contemporary luxury wear.

Add a Pinch of Coriander

THAI TOURISM IN NUMBERS

How much is it worth?

The contribution by businesses linked to the travel and tourism sector to GDP and employment, percentage of the total, data for 2019–24 (tourism from China was almost wiped out during the pandemic but is now recovering) and forecast for 2034

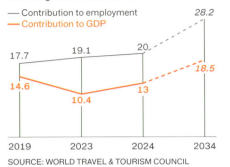

SOURCE: WORLD TRAVEL & TOURISM COUNCIL

Overtourism

Cities around the world with the most tourists per inhabitant, 2023

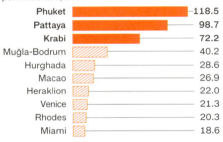

SOURCE: MONEYTRANSFERS

Sex tourism

$6.4 billion

the annual contribution of sex tourism to GDP in 2015 – according to a study by research institute Havocscope, which specialises in black markets – approximately 1.5% of GDP for that year.

SOURCE: HAVOCSCOPE

200–300,000

the estimated number of sex workers, of whom 70% come from rural areas; the average age of those entering the sector is 20–24.

SOURCE: GITNUX

Top destinations for Chinese tourists

Holidays arranged by Beijing travel agencies, 2023 (thousands)

SOURCE: ECONOMIST INTELLIGENCE UNIT

Medical tourism

Annual turnover from medical tourism around the world by country, 2020, in millions of $

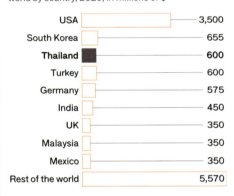

Price comparison for a selection of common medical procedures, 2022, in thousands of $

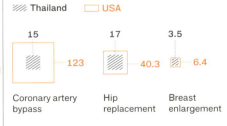

SOURCE: MYMEDITRAVEL

130   THE PASSENGER   Valeria Palermi

SEX TOURISM

Not included in the original Five Fs, nor in the subsequent expansion to eleven, sex tourism – for which the country is one of the world's most popular destinations – arguably contributes more to the image of Thailand abroad than any initiative the government might come up with. The sex industry was already well established when Thailand decided to host US bases and soldiers involved in the war in Vietnam, but there was an explosion during those years, and the reaction to its new visibility led to the criminalisation of prostitution in 1960, reinforced in 1996. The widespread belief that prostitution is 'tolerated' is simply not true: rather, the police earn so much from it in extortion and corruption that they have no interest in suppressing it, let alone seeing it legalised, as reformers proposed in 2023. The result is that the sex workers (an estimated 90 per cent of whom are women) have no form of legal protection or social security, as became abundantly clear during the Covid-19 pandemic. Nevertheless, in a society with attitudes that remain profoundly male-chauvinist, sex work – in bars, brothels and massage parlours in the red-light districts of Bangkok, Phuket and Pattaya – has long been normalised, is usually voluntary, carries little social stigma and leads to a certain redistribution of wealth towards rural areas, given that's where most of the sex workers, who send home a part of their earnings, come from. The situation for foreign workers is very different, unfortunately. They are often refugees, some of them underage and are victims of sex trafficking run by criminal organisations.

but I've got to admit that when he was in power he did a lot of good things. He's someone who makes things happen. They're getting some impressive experts involved in the committee now, and it's a good approach. If they manage to keep out pen-pushers and yes-men, it will work well. They want to look to the contemporary, even if they're scared of taking it too far.'

Narisa Chakrabongse again: 'Will the politicians be able to cope with the consequences? Will they be able to handle all the questions it might raise? Speaking as a publisher, I can say that we're not seen today as a culturally interesting country. Inequality and lack of freedom take too much of a toll. And also, many people abroad are full of ridiculous prejudices; all they respect about Thailand is our food. Maybe that's a problem for all countries with good food, beautiful women, historic sites and fantastic beaches: no one thinks that we can carry intellectual weight, too. That's also the case in Italy, right? We're just seen as a holiday destination and taken less seriously than other countries. But I think that Thailand really can exercise soft power, particularly when it comes to LGBTQ+ rights, especially now with the equal-marriage law. Trans people have always been accepted here; they're an integral part of our society. That's something very positive about Thai culture.'

Srettha Thavisin had also thought of this when he was prime minister. He proposed Bangkok and Phuket as possible venues for an international LGBTQ+ summit in 2028, 'to show the world the country's support for gender inclusivity'. If this goes ahead Thailand will become the first country in Asia to host the summit, described by Srettha Thavisin as 'the World Cup' for the LGBTQ+ community.

A Country With No Refugees

NICHA WACHPANICH
Translated by Noh Anothai

A group of Burmese arrive from Palu, Myawaddy, eastern Myanmar, in December 2021. Thousands of civilians from the region have been forced to flee to Thailand following attacks by the Burmese military on the Karen National Union (KNU).

In Thailand refugees do not exist – at least, not officially. However, a flood of exiles, primarily from Myanmar, are finding refuge from persecution in the country. But with its chauvinistic policies, bureaucratic absurdities and shortage of labour, Thailand has an ambiguous attitude towards immigration.

Something you need to know before going to Thailand – as essential as knowing how to say 'less spicy' when ordering food – is the fact that when Thais yell 'Hey, come and eat!' as you pass by, this is merely a customary greeting. It does not mean you actually need to join them. OK, you *could* join them, but the person who issued the invitation might be a bit flummoxed since, generally speaking, these words are the equivalent of asking 'How are you?' in English. You could rack your brains about how best to condense into a simple answer all the trials and tribulations you are currently undergoing, but in reality the person who asked wanted no such response. Yet this is how we greet each other. Thai culture is a culture of eating. But whereas soft power has exported foods such as pad Thai and mango sticky rice all over the world, in reality Thai cuisine is much more diverse – and Thailand more of a melting pot – than we might think.

On the menu today are yellow peas with roti and a spicy aubergine dip along with sweet, milky tea.

Come, come and eat.

THE SCENT OF BURMESE TEA

'*Thamin sabibila*?' I shout to the tall, skinny man seated in front of the shop smoking a cigarette.

He breaks into a smile, the cigarette still held in one corner of his mouth. 'No, I haven't eaten yet,' he responds in Thai, although I addressed him in Burmese. We launch into a conversation in English. Neither of us knows much of each other's native language except for a few basic survival phrases used to break the ice.

Here, in this two-storey shophouse along a sidestreet where only the occasional motorbike passes by, customers are slowly coming in for breakfast before getting their days started. As he waits for his tea, Thet Swe Win, the thirty-something owner, tells me about the heated conversation that took place here the previous afternoon. Over cups of sweet, strong tea a group of young men were engaged in a debate no less intense than the tea. Some were taking to task their government-in-exile, the National Unity Government of Myanmar (NUG), while others were defending its politicians for putting pressure on foreign

NICHA WACHPANICH is a Bangkok-based journalist who specialises in environmental issues and human rights. She regularly visits migrant communities near the Thailand–Myanmar border as well as those in the industrial zones of Thailand. She is a contributor to HaRDstories and works with the Democratic Voice of Burma and the Myanmar-focused Visual Rebellion collective.

> 'The ethnic armed organisations welcomed these young men and women from the cities, providing room, board and military training – and creating a generation convinced that armed struggle can cast off the military's yoke.'

leaders not to support the junta that had taken control of the country. It was a shame that I hadn't been able to join in; although the debate had likely been all in Burmese, I would have had fun cheering.

Thet is proud to serve his tea to everyone from whichever end of the political spectrum: a sweet, hot, milky tea for twenty-five baht ($0.70) to be drunk alongside authentic Burmese fare.

This is not the Republic of the Union of Myanmar, however, but Mae Sot, a border town in the far northwest of the Kingdom of Thailand – although the two are a mere river crossing apart. Mae Sot is now full of Burmese-style tea houses, particularly since 2021 when many sprouted up to meet the influx of Burmese into this little town.

Myanmar is known for having the longest civil war in history, starting the day it declared its independence from the British Empire in 1947. It was then that Myanmar's largest ethnic group, the Bamars, seized power, transforming this country of over 135 ethnicities into a battlefield, and the country has remained entrenched in military rule to this day. All this has been despite the numerous attempts at building peace, which culminated in 2010 when the country held a general election and opened its doors to investors for the first time in decades. But just as it seemed as if democracy was taking root – after the National League for Democracy, led by the iconic Aung San Suu Kyi, won by a landslide in 2015 – the military flouted the election results and staged yet another coup in 2021.

The people took to the streets. Unrest spread through all sections of society: students, artists, civil servants and private-sector workers and even some uniformed officers joined in a civil disobedience movement that aimed to undermine the establishment of yet another military regime. But the army responded with violence, and live ammunition soon replaced rubber bullets as the main means of dispersing protesters.

'I was at an NGO working on Buddhist–Muslim relations in the country,' Thet tells me, recalling his days in Yangon, the former capital and one of the most developed cities in Myanmar. 'Anyone who questioned the state was a target, even if you hadn't gone out on to the protest stage to rally the crowds yourself.'

Thet did what many city dwellers did in order to survive: he fled into the jungle, into those areas controlled by the various ethnic armed factions that have long been in conflict with the central government. The ethnic armed organisations welcomed these young men and women from the cities, providing room, board and military training – and creating a generation convinced that armed struggle can cast off the military's yoke.

Thet lived in the jungle for six months before deciding to flee to Thailand, trekking through dense forest and following in the footsteps of those who had shared his ideals before him as well as

Above: Ma Su Lwin, a Burmese migrant worker, with her son, born during the Covid-19 pandemic. After the factory she worked in closed down, she couldn't afford to pay medical fees to give birth and to raise her child, so she moved to Thailand.
Below: Burmese migrant workers in a rice paddy in Mae Sot, Thailand.

SCAM CITIES

A new type of criminal activity is spreading across Southeast Asia. According to a 2024 report by the United States Institute of Peace (USIP), *Transnational Crime in Southeast Asia*, 'transnational criminal networks emanating predominantly from China' are targeting 'millions of victims around the world with illegal and unregulated online gambling and sophisticated scamming operations. As of the end of 2023, a conservative estimate of the annual value of funds stolen by these syndicates approached $64 billion.' The cybercrime hubs exist in what Jason Tower, director of USIP's Burma programme, calls 'special criminal zones'. The heart of darkness lies within a radius of a few dozen kilometres of Myawaddy, in Myanmar, across the border from Mae Sot, the westernmost city in Thailand. There are fifteen 'scam cities', where tens of thousands of people work like slaves. According to Interpol this human trafficking involves between 75,000 and 250,000 people. They are IT professionals and experts in marketing and e-commerce, recruited with the promise of excellent earnings. After spending time in places like the UAE, they find themselves in border towns like Shwe Kokko, held prisoner in hotels and apartment blocks that were closed during the Covid-19 pandemic, converted and fortified. They can be seen from the Thai side, ten or so kilometres north of Mae Sot. Those who rebel are tortured. Those who try to escape are killed. The other victims are millions of people all around the world who fall prey to what is known as 'pig butchering': they are 'fattened up' with fake opportunities before being 'butchered'. (M.M.)

many of Myanmar's working class, who for decades had stolen through those same woodlands to work illegally in Thailand. Thet lived in a kind of limbo, having nothing on his person except his linen *longyi* as he waited for a human smuggler to pick him up. To get across, a smuggler first has to find a spot where one ethnic group holds both banks of the river – a river brown with silt, the colour of milky tea.

Our drinks arrive at the table, and Thet inhales deeply. The steam swirls with his memories.

'Before, I used to come to Thailand every few months to take part in various conferences, but that was the first time I'd snuck across the border,' he tells me, his voice deep. 'It was so different that it made me question my very being.'

The moment he stepped across the Thai border he felt that the rest of his life would never be the same. He had come without a visa. Thailand allows Burmese tourists to stay in the country on a thirty-day free visa if they come by air and fourteen days if by land, but passing through checkpoints controlled by the Burmese government had not been an option for Thet. He hid himself beneath sacks of rice and clandestinely crossed the border that separates Myanmar and Thailand for more than two thousand kilometres.

'In merely crossing the border I became an illegal entity. I could get arrested at any time,' he says. 'But, just as easily, if I went back across the river I'd be legal again. Legal, illegal – what do these words mean really? People like me, we aren't murderers. We haven't killed anyone. We only crossed the river to save our lives.'

Although the two countries have shared a history stretching back hundreds of years, Thailand's diplomatic stance towards Myanmar is ambiguous. Despite the recent turmoil, the Thai government still smiles on its counterpart in Myanmar, on many occasions even lending the junta support. At the same time it also turns a blind eye to insurgents and other political refugees like Thet residing in Thailand.

But, in any case, even if they have escaped retaliation or execution in Myanmar, these are not 'refugees' who live in Thailand but members of the general workforce, tourists, businesspeople and students. Like other countries in Southeast Asia, Thailand has never ratified the United Nations charter on the status of refugees – fearing, perhaps, the legal constraints this would entail and lacking the resources to dedicate to such people. This gives those who have entered Thailand illegally only one choice for normalisation: to apply for the legalisation programme administered by Thailand's Ministry of Labour. Thailand officially has no refugees, but the truth is that there may be more than a million.

Thet sets his teacup down and shows me his immigration card – after living as an illegal alien for so long, in constant fear of the police and spending most of his time hidden in different rented rooms, today he is at last a legal resident in Thailand. Looking at his pink card we might see a life circumscribed by a single job title – the card classifies him as a construction worker – but if we strip away the costume in which the law has dressed him, we would see a man who speaks English well, who comes from a middle-class family, who has earned his master's degree and won international recognition for his work in human rights.

'Yes, I am a refugee,' he laughs lightly, the word unfamiliar in his mouth. 'I have fled from danger to be here. I can't go anywhere else – not to Burma nor to a third country.'

Thet chooses not to seek asylum, which would allow him to move to the West, but to remain in Thailand, next to his homeland, while his wife has gone abroad with their children to continue their studies.

Living without dignity in Thailand, what can he do but help his compatriots? In this little town Thet runs a safe house for those in similar circumstances. The United Nations estimates that altogether more than two million people have fled Myanmar since the political turmoil of 2021. Similarly, Thai social organisations estimate that around a thousand refugees enter Thailand for political as well as economic reasons every day.

Although particulars change, everyone is looking for the same things: a home and security. Once the storm in his life began to calm down Thet decided to raise what funds he could and in 2022 convinced the inhabitants of his safe house to open a tea shop. They called it Loot Lat Yay – the Freedom Café.

Tea houses are central to Burmese culture. They are where people meet their friends to talk about football, the economy, politics. As well as food, the Freedom Café also gives space to other activities, such as debating and chess.

'I want to run a tea house as a safe space, a place people can call home or, at least, where they can get a taste of what was home, even if only for a moment,' Thet says.

I have never been to Yangon, don't know what a tea house in Myanmar is really like, but I believe that in this they must be successful.

A MOUTHFUL OF PE PYOTE

Besides fulfilling a social function, the other reason Thet opened his tea house was practical: with life in their new country starting to come together, the thirty inmates of Thet's house started getting on each other's nerves. Thet thought the time had come. 'They needed something to keep them busy, something meaningful to do with their lives,' he says, 'so they wouldn't just be refugees sitting around at home doing nothing.'

These two young people, both around twenty years old, from Yangon and Mandalay, Myanmar, joined the People's Defence Force in Lay Kay Kaw. Following a military raid on their city they are now hiding in a safe house in Thailand.

Saying this, he calls his cook from the kitchen to show what she has prepared for us.

Although Burmese food is diverse, I like simple dishes like *pe pyote* the most: dried yellow peas, boiled and mashed then seasoned fairly sweet so you can dip some freshly baked flatbread into it, still warm from the clay oven.

'In Yangon people mostly live in shop-houses several storeys high. When they hear hawkers going down the streets shouting *Pe pyote, pe yoooteeeeee!* they'll lower baskets from their windows,' explains Lin, smiling. 'My mum used to tell me that if I didn't do well at school that one day I'd be selling *pe pyote*.' The young woman clarifies that she doesn't look down on anyone who sells such delicious food for a living, but this porridge of boiled peas is an affordable food

A Country With No Refugees 139

that anyone can buy, so *pe pyote* vendors tend to earn little – something of which this former nurse's mother liked to remind her.

A college-educated woman who once worked at a state hospital, now Lin sells *pe pyote* in a Thai frontier town.

The *coup d'état* upended life in Myanmar for everyone, not just those behind the walls of parliament. Thousands of civil servants and public administrators joined the civil disobedience movement, refusing to work so they could take a position against the military's establishment of itself as government. With its teachers, police officers, doctors, clerks and even many soldiers engaged in silent but powerful protest, the state was crippled.

Lin had loved her job and her patients, but she chose to engage in her own civil disobedience a week after the coup. Like the others, she found popular support for the civil disobedience movement (CDMers, as the dissidents were called) right across Burmese society. But staging a revolution is not like slicing a vegetable – one clean cut and it's done. It dragged on longer than anyone could have imagined. Initially, Lin received a small sum of money, equivalent to about $54 a month, from the local community, which supported activists like her. But as the fourth anniversary of the *coup* approached, even this small stipend dwindled as everyone had to attend to their own survival.

Lin had to find work. She had heard that Thailand was well known for its medical tourism and that it received travellers from around the world seeking not only quality but also relatively affordable medical services. The young nurse thought she stood a chance of finding an opportunity. Her dream was dashed, however, when she received her papers; they listed her as a worker in a textile factory.

Thai law reserves at least seventeen professional categories exclusively for Thai nationals, ostensibly because in these sectors Thailand still needs to improve in order to keep up with other countries. For the most part these fall under skilled work, including medical services. But therein lies the irony. In 2005 the World Health Organization classified Thailand as an ageing society. Thai leaders have since been bemoaning the dwindling workforce, especially of skilled workers. In Thailand the doctor-to-patient ratio is 1:1,680, with most healthcare professionals concentrated in urban areas. Meanwhile, neighbouring countries such as Myanmar have a ready supply of young men and women who flee across the border in droves, precisely to those border towns that suffer from a lack of medical personnel.

In the sweltering heat of April 2024, after the traditional Southeast Asian New Year celebrations, Myanmar's military brought in compulsory conscription for men (between the ages of eighteen and thirty-five) and women (from eighteen to twenty-seven) and those in specialist professions, such as doctors, up to the age of forty-five.

'A college-educated woman who once worked at a state hospital in Myanmar, now Lin sells *pe pyote* in a Thai frontier town.'

'Our head chef is a former nurse. Our waiter led the student protests at his school.' So Thet introduces his staff to me. 'As for our regular customers, one of them used to fight in the People's Army, where he was wounded and left disabled. He likes to come here to debate with a former tattoo artist who now works picking corn.'

Even though they had no previous experience managing a restaurant, they have learned quickly. Lin is trying out new menu items. She has an income, and it feels better than sitting in the safe house doing nothing, but she still misses nursing. Every day she and the other staff hand out tea and pastries among student organisers and government workers engaged in civil disobedience who are less fortunate than themselves, who have not yet been able to find their own feet in this new country. Almost all of their clientele is Burmese except for a few Westerners who volunteer as teachers at the refugee camps not far from town. Along a stretch of border hemmed in by rivers and mountains there are nine camps. Although the Thai government does not formally recognise their status, it has nevertheless arranged temporary shelters for refugees in accordance with humanitarian principles. Most of them belong to the ethnic minorities that populate Myanmar's rural areas. Many of them are also in the long process of waiting to receive refugee status in another country. This can take anything from two to ten years.

Thailand's leaders – like everyone else – are unable to estimate how much longer the war might continue. These 'temporary' shelters that were first raised on the Thai border more than thirty years ago in 1988 – following the first major upheaval in Myanmar – are

today home to over 96,000 people. Thirty years corresponds to the time it takes for someone to grow from newborn to adult: a generation. For those who were born and raised here the word 'camp' does not refer to a summer retreat in the mountains but to life itself. Each camp has its own special regulations, like a world sealed in a bubble. Here they learn Burmese and English and do not really engage in Thai society. Some of the refugees' children and grandchildren want to go back and start lives in their homeland. Others feel no connection to it and wish to stay in Thailand.

Lin has never been to those camps, but she understands what life in limbo is like: unable to go back, unable to move forward, but stuck in between, as waiting turns into a lifetime.

I tell the tea house staff about a Japanese restaurant in Bangkok that offered, as a special menu item for its urban clientele, mushrooms grown in the camps

stir fried in butter. Perhaps because the restaurateur had grown up in the cultural melting pot of post-war Japan these refugee-camp mushrooms had been served alongside *musubi* topped with American Spam straight from the can. Even though the promotion had not lasted very long, at least it was able to help refugees who had not yet received work permits make a bit of money.

'But whatever money we earn we give to the police,' the nurse complains in broken English. Burmese people are often stopped by Thai police officers on the way to market. Sometimes they're threatened with extradition to Myanmar or given other reasons to be fined even if they have all their documents in order.

'My hope is that we can contribute to Thai society or the Thai economy. We want to,' Thet says. 'We've seen both the good and bad in Thailand, but we love this country. If we could do something for it while we're here, it would be good for both the Burmese and the Thai communities.'

A PLATE OF KASHKE BADEMJAN
Five hundred kilometres from the tea shop on the border, lights illuminate the Bangkok night. In Thong Lor, one of the city's financial and nightlife districts, a table laden with flowers and Middle Eastern dishes prompts me to get my phone out to take photographs.

Fine-dining etiquette calls for chefs to come out of their kitchens to greet their customers, introduce their dishes and reveal the cooking techniques and inspiration behind them. This evening, however, the two Iranian chefs who crafted the food spread before us are not

present, sending a Thai representative out instead.

'Tonight, dinner will consist of eight courses,' she tells us, her rosy lips smiling. 'The side dish is not commonly found at Persian restaurants in Thailand. It's a favourite of the chef's: *kashke bademjan*.'

At her invitation I break off a piece of bread and dip it into a puree of spicy aubergine topped with fresh mint and *kashke*. I'm happy that Sara, the chef, chose to prepare her favourite dish for us rather than other signature dishes, because today is an important day for her. Even though they are not present here to welcome us, she and her sous chef Alec have cooked their story into these dishes.

After being released from the international detention centre, Sara and Alec had searched for a way to support themselves. The forty-year-old Iranian woman took part in Click Aroi, a programme administered by Asylum Access Thailand, which takes small groups of urban refugees, trains them in cooking and food preparation and develops a

Above: Migrant workers in one of the hundreds of garment factories that have opened in Mae Sot, Thailand, and the surrounding areas. Many struggle with low wages and late payments but are afraid to stand up for their rights with their employers.

Opposite: Burmese children help their parents work at a dump in Mae Sot. Many migrants are forced to live without papers and have to deal with language barriers. They have limited access to decent jobs or education for their children, who end up working in poor conditions as child labourers and are often paid less than the legal minimum.

A Country With No Refugees

menu of their national dishes to sell online. The association also hosts a 'refugee dinner' on the last Saturday of every month with all proceeds going to the refugees themselves.

'I learned to cook after getting married. My mother taught me,' Sara had said when I'd met her a month before this dinner. But since refugee status is sensitive information that can have legal repercussions, she does not divulge her status openly and certainly not here at a public dinner. Instead, we learned about the circumstances of each other's lives on a different occasion.

Tall, slender and looking very Middle Eastern, Sara and Alec stand out among the local Thais, but the latter are probably not surprised to see them in their capital city, where foreigners are everywhere, as tourists, businesspeople and, more secretively, those here for their safety.

Their love has undergone many trials. Getting married in their country of origin was not easy since both are Catholics, a minority group in the Islamic Republic of Iran, where there are only an estimated 1.2 million Christians out of eighty-nine million people. A turning point came for the couple in 2018. Alec was working in a travel agency while studying at the only university in the city. In a class for his tourism sciences degree, each student was asked to make a presentation about an Iranian attraction of their choice. Alec chose Vank Cathedral, an Armenian church in Isfahan. Before a room full of hundreds of students, images of a mosque-like building appeared but with spires like Christian churches, and Alec selected a verse from the Bible to read.

'The following day a university official knocked on our front door and summoned me for interrogation. He demanded, "Don't you know this is an Islamic university? Don't you know you are in Iran?"' So Alec recalled for me as if it had happened only yesterday. 'I asked my neighbours to tell Sara that I would call her, and they told her and the rest of our building that I had been taken by our Muslim brothers.'

Twenty-three days in a re-education camp at an unspecified location – the tall, slender man whose demeanour was that of a teacher summarised them for me: 'They could even make you forget your own mother's name.' Although a serious matter, Alec had interspersed his story with smiles. His style was engaging, inviting us to ask questions, after the manner of someone who has taught for more than six years. (Since moving to Thailand, he has taught Persian at a private school.)

As soon as Alec had been released, friends applied for visas and bought tickets for him and Sara. It all happened so quickly. Within the space of a few hours the couple found themselves in a land neither of them had ever imagined living in.

In her free time Sara enjoys painting on leather in a Persian style, while on Sundays the couple attends mass. Although its population is predominantly Buddhist, Thailand is fairly open-minded about religion. I asked Sara if she likes it here.

'In Thailand we've gone through both good and bad like everybody else,' she said. Then suddenly her eyes welled up with tears. 'But when our passports expired – that's when everything fell apart.'

Alec had found employment at a university, but when an official processed his work permit for renewal he was told he would have to return to Iran

BAMBOO DIPLOMACY

'Once, the Chinese pulled rickshaws for rich Thais. Now, the Thais drive a Mercedes for rich Chinese,' complains one Thai nobleman. His nostalgic memories date back to the 1970s and 80s, back to a time when China was exhausted by the Cultural Revolution and the Soviet Union was trying to export its model to the whole of Southeast Asia. The kingdom was protected by the USA, and Thailand was the tile that could not fall in what was described as 'domino theory'. Then Chinese immigrants became Sino-Thais, and today they control many of the country's largest companies. China, the world's second-largest economy, is turning power relationships upside down: in 2023 it was the leading investor in Thailand. In October of that year then Prime Minister Srettha Thavisin met President Xi Jinping in Beijing, setting out new agreements in the strategic sectors of electric vehicles, semiconductors and the green economy. China reaffirmed its interest in megaprojects linked to its Belt and Road Initiative, such as the land bridge between the Gulf of Thailand and the Andaman Sea (see 'A Land Bridge' on page 76). China has also caught up with, if not overtaken, the USA in the military sphere, in terms of equipment sales and exercises. Thailand, however, continues to host Cobra Gold, one of the largest programmes of joint exercises with the US military. In spite of its tendency to align with China's pan-Asian policy, Thailand remains faithful to its concept of bamboo diplomacy, which is modelled on that plant's flexibility. (M.M.)

to complete the process. 'I missed Iran, but that would have been impossible.' Although there had been news that Iranian society had grown more tolerant in religious matters, yet the incarceration and death of a woman who refused to wear a *hijab* and the subsequent crushing of the demonstrations that followed convinced Alec that he would not be safe.

With no other choice, the couple went into hiding when their visas expired, until one day when they could no longer escape the law's reach. Again there was a knock at the door, and once more Alec – and this time Sara, too – found themselves behind bars. This time there was no torture of the kind that would make a prisoner 'forget his mother', but that does not mean their time in the international detention centre in Bangkok's Immigration Bureau was unmemorable. There, hundreds of people of different nationalities were crowded into dormitories, separated only by gender, and so Alec and Sara were kept apart. Neither had any idea how the other was getting on.

Day 1: Under a bright light kept on twenty-four hours a day, Sara lies awake, her eyes wide open.
Day 2: The food distributed is rice and cucumber soup.
Day 3: A British roommate is visited by an officer.
Day 4: The British roommate is allowed to leave.
Day 5: The inmates take a communal shower.
Day 10: ...
Day 12: A newcomer from Sudan. He says he has been granted refugee status by the UN and is about to move to Canada but must first serve his sentence for overstaying his visa in

STREET FOOD

When you read recommendations for the best street-food stalls in Bangkok, make sure they are up to date. Although Thai street food is regarded as being among the best in the world and constitutes one of the capital's attractions, the authorities consider it a sign of backwardness, disorder and dirt and in recent years have declared war on the sector. In 2017 there was even talk of a total ban, and the culinary landscape is, in fact, changing rapidly. In the meantime, many stallholders have been evicted. The declared aim is to make the pavements less crowded, chaotic and dirty through a restyling operation with a definite whiff of gentrification. According to official estimates, in 2023 there were over twenty thousand food traders in business, but half of them were no longer on the streets, having been relocated to purpose-built premises designed for catering outlets. The model being followed is that of the hawker centres of Singapore, a city that serves as a role model of order and cleanliness. In these centres, the street traders have to pay rent that is too high for many of them, while the customer base in some cases is smaller than it once was. Street food is not just a draw for tourists, however, it also plays an essential role for residents of the capital, because for many it is the only food they can afford or consume, given that many apartments have no kitchen. In a society of great inequality, the stalls are also one of the few places where different social classes mix.

Thailand. He is to stay one month until the day his flight leaves.
Day 15: ...
Day 20: A Burmese inmate tells Alec that he has been here for five years.
Day 25: Celebrate Christmas Day with cucumber soup. Sara performs her normal routine: pray and cry.

The Iranian embassy sent no one to help the couple. Alec believes that because of the various conflicts that broke out in the Middle East in 2024 their plight was not deemed a priority.

Although the international detention centre is located inside Bangkok's Immigration Bureau surrounded by busy food stalls and close to a public park, few Thais are aware of what befalls the foreigners who spend time in the centre. Although some human rights activists and progressive politicians have encouraged the Thai government to improve conditions inside the centre, the issue is not one of the Thai public's most pressing concerns.

On the thirtieth day Alec and Sara stepped out of the detention centre, their bodies shaking. They had been contacted by an international organisation that assists refugees and only in this way had been made aware of a new Thai law which meant that to make bail they needed 130,000 baht ($3,527) and a Thai guarantor.

The day I met them, the Iranian couple were smartly dressed in clean clothes, but traces of terror were still evident in their eyes. Apart from the fear there was also hunger – they ate no more than two meals per day to keep spending down. They had borrowed money from every source they could to make bail and had hardly any to keep for themselves. Their new status as protected persons meant they were not allowed to work.

'I am a teacher, and she is an artist. I am ready to earn my own living and therefore cease to be a burden on the Thai government. If refugees were allowed to work we could pay taxes and stimulate the economy,' said the former language teacher. He doesn't think that he and his wife would be stealing jobs from Thais but rather that their work might be a point of interest for them.

'Although we've been released from detention, it still feels like we're stuck behind bars. We've had our rights taken from us. We have fewer every day.' Saying this Alec asked me to turn my arm over. 'What blood type are you?'

'Type O,' I replied, confused.

'And there it is. Your blood type and my religion are the same: we can't change them,' Alec said. 'Even though that day at the university brought us here, yet to declare before a large audience that Christians exist in Iran – this I'll never regret.'

After dinner I take the bus home. Here in Bangkok the traffic is so congested that it could take me hours. Along the way the bus passes Yaowarat Road, Bangkok's Chinatown, its streets and alleys full of stalls and lined with restaurants serving food that my friends and I regularly sample. Not far from here is Phahurat, the centre of the South Asian community, with more Indian restaurants than can be imagined. Both are neighbourhoods originally settled by immigrants to Thailand more than two hundred years ago. It's true that in some ways Thai society instils its people with nationalistic values, but there is no extreme anti-immigrant sentiment here. Deep down I think we are more ready to embrace being a melting point than we even know.

Thet's voice comes floating over to me above the braying of car horns. 'We are all of us only refugees for the time being, waiting for when we can return home.'

A Country With No Refugees

There Has Been Blood

The global thirst for palm oil has never been more ravenous. Caught in a stranglehold between the industry's needs and a multi-generational war waged on Thailand's poor, the farmers of some communities in the south of the country have banded together to defend their land rights.

DIANA HUBBELL

Somjed Jandang, a palm oil farmer, is one of the villagers from Klong Sai Pattana district in Surat Thani province who have been fighting for their land for more than a decade. Members of the community have been harassed and killed by the local mafia. Many believe that a palm oil company, Jiew Kang Jue Pattana Co. Ltd, which has illegally occupied a 217-hectare plot and planted oil palm trees, is behind the violence.

Surat Thani

It was the morning of 11 February 2015 when Somrudee Boonthonglek first saw the two men outside her shop. They were dressed as construction workers, with black masks that guarded their faces against the dust. Only their eyes were visible as they passed by on a motorbike. Around 6 p.m. that evening Somrudee was making dinner when the two men returned. Sauntering through the door of her shop, they asked to buy some beer. Somrudee's father, sixty-one-year-old Chai Boonthonglek, who had been attempting to soothe her crying six-month-old son, passed the child off to fetch the drinks. When he turned around, one of the men pulled out a .357 pistol and fired six shots, striking Chai in the head and torso. By the time the police arrived an hour later his body was cold.

'I was two steps away from my dad when they shot him. Then they just walked away and got on their motorbike like nothing happened,' Somrudee says. Her son, a rambunctious five-year-old who squirms in her lap as she speaks to me, has no memory of his grandfather.

'My dad loved this place so much, so I am staying here to fulfil his dream,' says Somrudee, now in her early thirties.

Since 2009 she has lived in Klong Sai Pattana, a 160-hectare farming community of seventy or so families in Surat Thani province in Southern Thailand. Klong Sai Pattana is the largest of five neighbouring communities that make up the Southern Peasants' Federation of Thailand (SPFT), an advocacy group for land rights. Most SPFT members are like Somrudee and her parents, Chai and Usa Suwannaphat, who followed her in 2011 – ordinary people who never owned much of anything, drawn by the promise of a plot of earth where they could grow enough food for themselves and their children. For Chai and Usa, after nearly thirty years together scraping by on labouring jobs and sorting through recyclables for pocket change, operating a tiny general store and having ten rai (about 1.6 hectares) to call their own felt like a small miracle.

For more than a decade three of SPFT's farming communities have been locked in brutal land disputes with oil palm plantations. Most of these plantations were created after a 1964 law allowed thirty-year farming concessions on state-owned land; these leases were initially given to powerful individuals, and after the concessions expired many

DIANA HUBBELL is a James Beard Award-winning American journalist who specialises in food and culture. Previously based in Bangkok, she has reported on Thailand for over a decade. She currently resides in New York, where she is an editor at *Atlas Obscura*. During her career she has contributed to the *Guardian*, *The Washington Post*, *Condé Nast Traveler*, *Wired*, the *Independent*, *Vice*, *Architectural Digest*, *Eater*, *Esquire*, *Travel + Leisure* and *Playboy*.

of the plantations remained or, in some cases, expanded well beyond their original legal borders. In 1997 one of Thailand's more transparent governments issued the Official Information Act, which enabled land rights activists to access troves of documents that proved the scale of the illegal occupations. A public outcry to redistribute some of the expired concession areas to the country's estimated eight million landless poor grew in the years that followed. In 2009, after a court case determined that one palm oil corporation, Jiew Kang Jue Pattana, had illegally occupied its land for decades, the plaintiff, the Agricultural Land Reform Office (ALRO), allowed a group of farmers from SPFT to settle in the area that is now Klong Sai Pattana. The community has existed in the shadow of Jiew Kang Jue Pattana's oil palm trees ever since, separated from the plantation by a narrow dirt road.

Jiew Kang Jue Pattana may not have had a right to the land, but multiple human rights groups say that the company showed no remorse about spilling blood to reoccupy it. According to the SPFT, between 2009 and 2018 the corporation kept up a steady stream of intimidation in an attempt to force the farmers to vacate Klong Sai Pattana, including bulldozing about sixty homes. Human rights groups also allege that gangsters hired by Jiew Kang Jue Pattana repeatedly fired automatic rifles into the village and killed four of the community's members, including Chai. Less than two years after his death more gunmen attacked Somrudee's husband, who escaped with a wounded arm and a pickup truck riddled with bullet holes.

After a court ordered Jiew Kang Jue Pattana to vacate the state-owned land entirely in 2018 the corporation officially folded. But there has been no justice for the people of Klong Sai Pattana – who are not the only community in SPFT's network to suffer violence and harassment. A short drive away, Santi Pattana and Khao Mai Pattana are also embroiled in conflicts with palm oil companies. On 20 October 2020 Dam Onmuang narrowly dodged a bullet when an attacker sneaked into Santi Pattana and fired at him at 1 a.m. while he was on security duty. Mary Lawlor, UN Special Rapporteur, and Agnes Callamard, the then-UN Special Rapporteur, released a letter implicating United Palm Oil Industry in the shooting. (United Palm Oil has not responded to a request for comment as of publication.) Dam, who is sixty-nine, says the attack has made him fearful of leaving his home and that his health has declined dramatically as a result. In August 2021 his attacker was convicted of attempted murder; it was the first time that any of SPFT's assailants suffered the legal consequences of their crimes.

The attacks on the villagers of SPFT are far from isolated incidents in the broader struggle over land rights in Thailand; at least seventy land rights lawyers and community activists have vanished or been confirmed dead over the past few decades. And Thai governments have often been less than sympathetic to the country's landless poor, particularly in the wake of the 2014 military *coup d'état*. The Thai government has not only turned a blind eye to the attacks but it has at times actively worked to displace peasants on behalf of oil palm plantations and other large agribusinesses. After initially promising that the farmers could remain in Klong Sai Pattana, ALRO has repeatedly threatened to redistribute the land

Funeral portraits of people who have been killed in Klong Sai Pattana district, Surat Thani province.

Bullet holes in Apichart's pickup, evidence of the occasion a gunman attempted to kill villagers in Klong Sai Pattana.

WAITING FOR SONGKRAN

The rainy season arrives more or less at the same time as Songkran, or Buddhist New Year, which falls on 13 April and is celebrated, not by chance, with water fights in the streets. This is the time of year when young palm trees are transplanted from the nurseries to the fields and rice is sown after the ploughing festival. Farmers are no longer the only ones who wait for the first storms with trepidation, however; in the cities the air has become increasingly unbreathable, and it is no longer enough, even for those who can afford it, just to shut yourself away at home with a purifier. In February and March Bangkok, and even more so Chiang Mai in the north, are covered by a dense, poisonous haze and start to rise up the charts of the world's most polluted places. In addition to the smog caused by intense traffic and industry, pollution comes from the controlled burning of crop residues in preparation for the crop planting, which causes a surge in PM 2.5 particles in the atmosphere to twenty times the limit deemed safe by the World Health Organization. In 2023, according to the Ministry of Health, more than ten million Thais needed treatment for pollution-related conditions. The government is studying ways to alleviate the problem, from cloud seeding – in an attempt to bring the rains earlier – to the electrification of the tuk-tuk fleet, Bangkok's iconic motorised rickshaws, to laws regulating crop burning, but so far, runs the joke among the people of Chiang Mai, the strategy still seems to be ... to wait for Songkran.

to corporate interests, according to the members of SPFT. (ALRO had not responded to a request for comment at the time of writing.) In 2017 more than a dozen members of the federation's Nam Daeng Pattana community were charged with criminal offences, including trespassing on a mining company's land; seven served jail sentences.

In the case of Chai's alleged assassin, the provincial court in Wiang Sa District of Surat Thani province ruled that it must have been too dark for Somrudee to see clearly and dismissed the charges without further investigation. Members of the community have urged Somrudee and Usa to flee, but they refuse to leave. Together they care for Somrudee's youngest son and the garden that Chai left behind. Usa knows there is little chance of justice for Chai, but she continues to tell his story. 'I lost my husband in the fight for this land,' she says. 'This is the land we fought for with our blood. We fight for it with our tears. This is where I have decided I want to die.'

*

Thailand has the eighth-largest economy in Asia, but its wealth gap is vast and ever widening. In 2016 the country had the third-highest economic inequality in the world, according to the Credit Suisse Global Wealth Report, with its fifty richest billionaires having a net worth equal to 30 per cent of the country's entire GDP. By the 2018 edition of the report Thailand had topped Russia and India for the greatest degree of wealth inequality in the world, with the top 1 per cent of the population owning 66.9 per cent of the country's wealth. That same year, 55 per cent of the population worked in the informal sector, many living one illness or missed pay cheque away from starvation; some 6.5 million people did not have enough to eat. Nearly a third of the population works in Thailand's agricultural sector, often as near-indentured servants to the corporations that control the land they tend. A 2020 report by the World Bank found that the number of agricultural workers earning less than the poverty line of ninety baht ($3) per day has been climbing since 2016.

In a country that relies heavily on agriculture land is everything, and nearly 80 per cent of the land in Thailand is controlled by just 20 per cent of the population. According to a 2019 case study conducted by Focus on the Global South, *Alternative Land Management in Thailand: A Study of the Southern Peasants' Federation of Thailand (SPFT)*: 'land ownership has become concentrated in the hands of a small number with access to information, capital, and connections to authorities'. ALRO, which is in charge of land distribution, is famously corrupt; its officials have historically made little effort to hide their interest in bribery. According to Pornpana Kuaycharoen, a coordinator at Land Watch Thailand, when many of the oil palm concessions were first handed out in the 1960s, anecdotal reports of bribery ran rampant, with local officials allegedly handing off parcels of land to powerful friends for as little as ten baht (33 cents) per rai (0.16 hectares).

After 22 May 2014, when Thailand's democratically elected prime minister was arrested during a *coup d'état* and the National Council for Peace and Order, a military junta under the leadership of General Prayut Chan-o-cha, seized power, inequality in Thailand steadily worsened. As prime minister until 2023, Prayut Chan-o-cha had an abysmal human rights record. During his time in power his administration eliminated political opposition and authorised the use of water cannon, tear gas and rubber bullets on crowds of civilian protestors in Bangkok. It also doled out hefty prison sentences for violations of the country's *lèse-majesté* law, which forbids anything that could be broadly interpreted as defamation of the monarchy – in multiple cases the crime in question was a Facebook post.

Less than a month after taking control, on 14 June 2014 the junta launched its Forestry Reclamation Policy, the stated purpose of which was to reforest a sizeable swathe of Thailand in order to combat global warming. Although the government claimed that this was an environmental initiative, activists say the goal was always to draw corporate investment to land that had been occupied by rural communities. Since 2015 more than eight thousand households faced forced eviction, while the Thai government leased out 999 hectares of the reclaimed land to agribusiness firms for growing oil palms, eucalyptus and rubber trees as well as to mining and cement companies. Those being forcibly removed have invariably been subsistence farmers, many of them Karen or other ethnic minorities. 'The Forestry Reclamation Policy allows for tremendous dispossession,' says Tyrell Haberkorn, a professor of Asian languages and cultures at the University of Wisconsin-Madison and the author of *In Plain Sight: Impunity and Human Rights in Thailand* (University of Wisconsin, 2019). '[The junta] argue it's to keep land from being further degraded, but if you look at who has been displaced and prosecuted, it's another way to target people who are already living in the margins of society'.

'Between 2014 and 2017 the Thai government brought 20,200 lawsuits against nearly 4,300 defendants, mostly on charges of trespassing in their own homes.'

According to Land Watch Thailand, between 2014 and 2017 the Thai government brought 20,200 lawsuits and criminal court cases against nearly 4,300 defendants, mostly on trumped-up charges of trespassing in their own homes. Soldiers have torched villages and marched elderly inhabitants off the land that they have farmed for generations at gunpoint. In one instance, near the beginning of the campaign in 2014, Brad Adams, Asia director at Human Rights Watch, described the areas to which more than a thousand villagers were forcibly relocated as 'uninhabitable'. Political propaganda and television commercials depict soldiers in full combat gear standing over unarmed villagers as though celebrating a heroic victory. 'What is happening in Thailand right now is nothing short of a war on the poor,' says Pranom Somwong, Protection International's representative in Thailand.

Since its foundation in 2008 in Surat Thani province, the SPFT has advocated for the landless poor, who seldom have a voice in Thai society. After an investigation by the Southern Poor People Network (SPPN) found that oil palm plantations were illegally occupying approximately 11,200 hectares of state-owned territory, mostly in the south of the country, members of SPFT moved into the disputed areas and began to work the land. From the beginning it was a bold social experiment, a radically democratic society struggling to survive within an increasingly authoritarian one. Among the organisation's principles are that anyone can lead, that all leaders must be elected by popular vote, that women should hold just as many positions of authority as men and that the communities should be good stewards of the environment for future generations. Every household of SPFT is entitled to an equal amount of land – ten rai (1.6 hectares) for planting crops and one rai (0.16 hectares) for building a home – provided they practise sustainable farming methods and sow a diverse mix of seeds. Community members are expected to take their responsibilities to the land and to one another seriously;

Tawat Ruengsri has been a palm oil farmer for almost ten years and is one of the community members trying to fight for their rights in a dispute with a palm oil company.

if they fail to do so they are asked to leave after a trial year. At the core of it all is a deep-rooted belief that everyone deserves to live with dignity, free from fear of hunger.

For Kusol Chuaywang that idea was immensely appealing. Although originally from Surat Thani province, she worked in Bangkok for many years as a contract driver for a van company. Each day, after she paid for fuel and the van's rental fee, she walked away with no more than 200 or 300 baht ($6 to $9). That left barely enough to cover the 2,000 baht ($63) she paid in monthly rent for an apartment on the outskirts of the capital. Decades of unchecked development – defined by a glut of luxury condos and high-end shopping malls – have rendered Bangkok effectively unliveable for workers like Kusol. After 2014 the Thai military junta accelerated the city's gentrification by supporting the displacement of lower-income neighbourhoods and reducing access to affordable food by destroying night markets and systematically evicting many of the city's 20,000-plus street-food vendors (see 'Street Food' on page 146). 'In the city I just survived day to day, nothing more. It was always a struggle to make ends meet,' Kusol says.

Kusol was in her late forties when she decided to begin a new life in Klong Sai Pattana. 'When we first started to cultivate the land, it was difficult. Most of us had to use our own savings [in the beginning],' she says. 'Now, there is always enough food … nobody has to worry about starving here.' Even at the height of the violence in those early years she was one of the few villagers who steadfastly refused to leave. 'My

Decha Nusong collects oil palm fruit after the harvest.

dream was to have my own land,' she says. 'Here I have hope.'

While SPFT members like Kusol joined to start over, for Surapol Songrak, an SPFT executive committee member, the movement for land rights is tied to a lifelong quest to build a more equitable society in Thailand. 'We believe that our struggle will free the land from the corporations and the billionaires and return it to the people,' he says. A round-faced man in his mid-fifties with wisps of salt-and-pepper hair, he speaks quietly but carries himself with an unmistakable air of authority. 'We are not the only group that has been fighting for justice and equality in this country, and we are not the first group to have lost our members,' he says. 'There are already several incidents in Thai political history of people's movements fighting against authoritarian powers. Each movement may look like it's the same, but the conflict evolves.'

The roots of that conflict in Thailand run back to the 1970s. It was a period of intense upheaval, one in which an authoritarian government brutally suppressed attempts at social and political reform. With the Cold War under way and communism spreading through other parts of Southeast Asia, paranoia among Thai landowners and government officials was running high. In 1972 security forces slaughtered as many as three thousand civilians in Phatthalung province who were accused of being communists. The incident came to be known as the *Thang Daeng*, or Red Drum Murders, since detainees were burned alive in

200-litre oil drums. Witnesses remember that soldiers revved the engines on their trucks to muffle the screaming. 'The official reason [for the violence] was to eradicate communism, but it extended further than that,' says Haberkorn, who publishes in English and Thai and writes about the incident in *Getting Away With Murder in Thailand: State Violence and Impunity in Phatthalung* (University of Kentucky Press, 2013). '"Communist" was defined as anything that was dissident, so it ended up including socialism, radical democracy and essentially any progressive political thought.'

Among those branded as social dissidents were the members of the Farmers' Federation of Thailand (FFT), an organisation founded in 1974 to advocate for the rights of landless peasants. Over the next five years many of the organisation's leaders were assassinated or simply disappeared. While some of the names of the victims were recorded by the National Human Rights Commission of Thailand, as with the Red Drum Murders, state records regarding the incidents remain sealed. Thailand's pattern of displacing rural communities and quashing resistance has continued through decades of regime changes. Between 1990 and 1992 the military launched a plan to evict up to five million residents, mostly in the country's rural northeast, and hand the majority of their land to commercial eucalyptus plantations. Phra Prachak Khuttasjitto, a former Buddhist monk, led the region's villagers in protest, wrapping trees in strips of saffron-hued fabric typically worn by monks as a form of symbolic ordination. In retaliation, soldiers arrested him, demolished houses and opened fire on crowds.

'Many other people lost their lives for the land,' Surapol says. He and SPFT's other leaders have taken lessons from past land rights movements in the hope that they can prevent history from repeating itself. The political players may have changed, but he sees numerous parallels to Thailand's past in terms of rising inequality and state-sanctioned violence. In some cases, even the methods of oppression mirror those dark times: when Porlajee Rakchongcharoen, a Karen human rights activist, vanished abruptly in 2014, the Department of Special Investigation (DSI) refused to investigate the disappearance. His burned remains were found five years later in an oil drum.

'The threat to equality, justice and who has access to land is similar across both times,' Haberkorn said. 'The difference with the rise of agribusiness is that the risk of ecological devastation is greater. In the '50s, '60s and '70s the primary risk was one of further entrenching inequality. Landowners back then weren't planting palm trees where they shouldn't be planted, and they weren't using as many toxic chemicals as today.' Among the pesticides still commonly used on Thailand's palm oil plantations is glyphosate, banned or restricted in a number of countries in North America and the EU, that one study found may increase the risk of developing non-Hodgkin lymphoma by 41 per cent. Although the Thai government took steps in 2019 to ban glyphosate – along with paraquat and chlorpyrifos, two highly toxic chemicals previously found on Thai oil palm plantations – it reversed the decision under pressure from the US government and Bayer. Workers on oil palm plantations and any villages downstream of their contaminated water supply suffer the

LITTLE FISH

If we turn our attention from the land to the sea, we see the same dynamics of predatory economies of scale: the big fish, or rather the big fishermen and fishing boats, eat the smaller ones. Fishing is a key sector in Thailand, employing more than two million people and accounting for almost 10 per cent of national exports, but in the 2010s a number of investigations carried out by journalists exposed overfishing practices, seafood fraud and the wretched conditions suffered by the 'sea slaves' employed on Thai fishing vessels. Under international pressure, the military junta in power at the time passed a law to expand crew registration and traceability of the catch, which is bearing its first fruits; fish stocks are recovering from the low point recorded in 2017, and the number of commercial fishing vessels has reduced by a quarter, while small fishing boats are reported to have doubled in number. The new business-friendly government that took power in 2023, however, is thinking of watering down the restrictions, causing alarm among environmentalists. The abundance of fish is not the only issue or factor to evaluate: stocks of one of the country's major sources of protein, mackerel, is reducing through the massacre of their fry perpetrated by trawling. Fishermen on the banks of the Mekong are also up in arms, as the construction of more than 160 dams has played havoc with the water levels, meaning the river is now populated by small fish with little market appeal.

effects. As has historically so often been the case the Thai government prioritised powerful corporate interests over the wellbeing of the poorest members of society.

*

Palm oil is the most consumed vegetable oil in the world, with nearly 10 per cent of the globe's permanent crop land dedicated to its production. As agricultural products go it is astonishingly versatile. In its unrefined form, red palm oil has a rich, intensely earthy flavour that is essential to cuisines from West Africa to Brazil. When processed, palm oil gives ice cream its scoopable, luscious texture, keeps peanut butter from separating and ensures that chocolate melts in your mouth, not in your hand. As a shelf-stable fat, solid at room temperature, it's an invaluable component of most processed foods. After June 2018, when the US instituted an official ban on partially hydrogenated oils, or trans fats (joining a number of other countries that had already restricted their use or banned them altogether), the use of palm oil as a substitute soared, and it now appears in about half of all products on grocery store shelves. Palm oil is also a key component in cosmetics, shampoos, bioplastics and biofuels, driving global consumption from sixteen million metric tonnes in 1996 to 60.7 million in 2017; if the industry continues on its current trajectory, palm oil consumption could quadruple again within the next thirty years.

While there is a growing demand for ethically sourced palm oil, much of the current supply chain is mired in human rights abuses. Indonesia and Malaysia together put out 85 per cent of the world's supply. Their economies depend heavily on the commodity, the low-cost production of which has been incentivised both domestically and by globalist financial institutions like the International Monetary Fund, which views it in part as a poverty eradication scheme. The resulting environmental devastation – it is a key driver of deforestation worldwide – and rampant human rights violations, which include trafficking, slavery, child labour and widespread sexual assault, have been well documented in both countries. 'There is a high demand for palm oil in processed foods and other consumer products primarily because it has been grown so cheaply,' says Robin Averbeck, the agribusiness campaign director at Rainforest Action Network. 'That low price point comes largely as a result of palm oil corporations stealing land from rural communities and labour from workers.'

For more than five decades the Thai palm oil industry has been marred by rampant exploitation, violence and corporate greed. Thailand is the world's number-three producer of palm oil. Although almost all of its crop is meant for domestic consumption, the Thai government has invested heavily in biodiesel and views palm oil as the key to energy independence, with production ramping up steadily since the mid-1970s. Unlike Malaysia and Indonesia, where large corporations dominate the palm oil industry, Thailand has hundreds of smaller plantations that employ approximately 300,000 workers in total.

Harvesting the crop is notoriously dangerous labour. The fruits grow on the tops of trees that can reach more than twenty metres high. Workers stand on the ground with thin metal poles and attempt to dislodge the oil palm fruits, each of which sports a spike-encrusted shell, weighs ten to twelve kilos and falls with such ample kinetic force that it can kill a man. Dam Onmuang – the SPFT member who was shot at in 2020 – once saw a tree fall and crush a fellow worker to death on an oil palm plantation.

Originally from the part of Surat Thani province where Santi Pattana is now, Dam was forced to leave after United Palm Oil Industry Public Co. Ltd illegally muscled into his village in 1976, setting fire to their crops and rice supplies. Desperate to feed his children, he took up logging, clearing forest land and other jobs for another oil palm plantation, often for as little as 100 baht ($3) a day. 'At that time, there were five members in my family. I have three children, my wife and me. It was not enough to live on,' he says. '[My children] were not starving, but it was not a pleasant life. We were very poor.' Like Dam, those who have chosen to work for substandard wages on the oil palm plantations often find themselves trapped in what some describe as modern-day serfdom with no hope of social advancement. Wages hover around 0.50 baht (2 cents) per kilo of fruit picked. On a good day a team of three might collect 1,000 to 1,500 kilos, meaning each person walks home with 200 baht ($6) or less, below even Thailand's modest minimum wage of – depending which province you are in – between 330 and 370 baht ($9.50–11) per day.

In 2008, the year SPFT was founded, oil palm plantations occupied 320,000 hectares of land. Since a government policy was established to expand the oil palm industry in 2005, that has risen steadily, particularly in the south. The current regime has plans to increase it by an additional 50 per cent by 2026. If that happens, SPFT's already precarious position is guaranteed to worsen.

Since 2010, when gunmen allegedly

hired by Jiew Kang Jue Pattana came through Klong Sai Pattana at dusk and murdered fifty-three-year-old Somporn Pattaphum, members of the community have lived under constant threat of attack or eviction. When that first death failed to scare residents away the violence escalated. By 2012 Klong Sai Pattana had become a war zone. Often, before the sun went down, villagers saw men in military-style camouflage gear or black clothes running into the bushes near the edge of their territory. After dark the farmers huddled in a bunker while bullets thudded into the earthen walls. No one knew which direction they were coming from or if they would stop. Members who patrolled the area around the bunker learned to find their way without the luxury of electric light for fear of being seen. 'Every night I heard gunshots. We had to be careful.

We had to be in a state of constant alert. We had to travel in groups,' Kusol says. Even during this time she volunteered to stand guard, walkie-talkie in hand in case of trouble. 'Sometimes when I had the night shift, I could tell from the shots that the attackers were right by us.'

As the death toll continued to rise in Klong Sai Pattana the Thai government continued to expand the palm oil industry, both by seizing land from villagers and by spending billions of baht on cash subsidies for plantation owners. In 2014, not long after the coup, Colonel Sombat Prasarnkasem of the Surat Thani Provincial Internal Security Operations Command stormed into Klong Sai Pattana with fifty soldiers carrying assault rifles. Without a search warrant, the military officers began interrogating members of SPFT. The officers forced Prateeb Rakmangthong, Klong Sai Pattana's leader, to the ground with an M-16 pressed against him and his hands tied behind his back, then demanded that he and the other farmers of Klong Sai Pattana vacate. When describing the incident later Prateeb would say that he felt like a prisoner of war. He admits that he was afraid, but he knew that if the farmers left Klong Sai Pattana they would have little hope of returning, so they had no choice but to ignore the order.

*

From an aeroplane Surat Thani province resembles a patchwork quilt of spiky palm fronds and spindly, silver-trunked rubber trees stretching to the horizon in orderly rectangular plots. In July, at the height of Thailand's rainy season, I climb into a pickup truck with Sutharee Wannasiri, a human rights activist and translator (who translated

'LAND' OF THE ARTISTS

The Land is a place where Thai and international artists and students live and work, producing not just works of art but rice, fruit and vegetables. It was founded in 1998 by the artists Rirkrit Tiravanija and Kamin Lertchaiprasert, who met in New York and were reunited in Chiang Mai. They had a shared desire to activate a space for experimentation in which artistic and environmental practices were in dialogue. In Sanpatong, twenty minutes from Chiang Mai, amid the paddy fields and tropical vegetation, you can find eccentric constructions such as Philippe Parreno and François Roche's *Battery House*, Mit Jai Inn's house hidden among the teak trees and the treehouse created by Thasnai Sethaseree and Robert Peter, to mention just a few. The paddy fields and agricultural land are cultivated in accordance with the philosophy of the Thai farmer Chaloui Kaewkong, who sees The Land as a human body, with the same ratio between its water content (60 per cent) and solid mass (40 per cent). Everything is done by trial and error, governed by the ingenuity and imagination of inhabitants and guests – an unusual approach that fits in with the spirit of The Land, where there are no rules to follow. Since the 1990s Tiravanija has been creating 'relational' works: he cooked and served pad Thai at the Paula Allen Gallery in New York, installed table-tennis tables and created life-size habitable replicas of his apartment – all examples of his desire to conjure up different ways of living that are less obsessed with art objects and more open to dialogue and participation. (Lorenza Pignatti)

the Thai material in this article), to visit the members of Klong Sai Pattana. Jugkarawoot Thuwaratkeeri, an SPFT member, cranks the ignition, and we set off down the dirt road that marks the boundary between Surat Thani and Krabi province. On either side of the divide is row upon row of evenly spaced oil palm trees planted by Jiew Kang Jue Pattana.

At one point the car stops, and Jugkarawoot points to a stretch of sun-dappled road. It was here that on 19 November 2012 villagers from Klong Sai Pattana found the bodies of two women from the community – Pranee Boonrat (fifty) and Montha Chukaew (fifty-four) – ringed with assault-rifle shells. Our vehicle slows down as we approach a raised bamboo hut that stands watch over the entrance to Klong Sai Pattana. Everyone who enters the community must pass one of these four guard stations, and no one is allowed in or out after 6 p.m. After a motion from our driver, the watchman on duty swings open the wooden gate. As we exit the truck a pack of skinny stray dogs greets us with lolling tongues and wagging tails.

Seated across a table laden with platters of bamboo-smoked sticky rice and fried bananas with a syrupy glaze is Prateeb. Now in his sixties, Klong Sai Pattana's elected leader has been involved in Thailand's fight for land justice for decades. According to Protection International there was once a bounty of 300,000 baht ($9,500) out for his assassination. 'In the past many land rights groups were not able to hold on to the land in the long run. We want others to see that we are the alternative,' Prateeb says. 'The constant threats and intimidation tactics were part of our decision to network. The landless and the poor should have the right to community. We believed that if we are united we are more powerful when we speak.'

Prateeb and the other leaders of SPFT have met with dozens of journalists, human rights activists and politicians at this table. There is always food present at these meetings, both as a gesture of hospitality and as a canny PR manoeuvre: while some Thai politicians who have visited in recent years, including the minister of agriculture, initially balked at eating 'peasant' food, the experience of sitting down for a meal together changed the conversation. A crucial legal component of land ownership in Thailand is that the land must be used; a heaping table is proof that the people of Klong Sai Pattana have transformed the soil, once depleted by the oil palm plantation's heavy use of pesticides, into fertile farmland. Dragon fruits, bananas, durians, lemongrass, cassava and more vegetables than I can name now grow here. The farmers have also experimented with coffee trees as well as a variety of mountain rice that does not require paddies. Some of the plants grow in orderly patches, while others crop up seemingly at random.

Virtually everything is edible, as I learn later while walking with one of the community's sustainable-farming leaders, Nittha Noosoma, a sharp-eyed woman in her thirties with a bob cut and a T-shirt depicting Uncle Sam that reads DOWN WITH AMERICAN IMPERIALISM. At one point Nittha hands me a fistful of cashew leaves, explaining that SPFT's core belief in food sovereignty means that everyone has the right to food that is safe; it's OK to snack directly from the ground because the community strictly prohibits the use of pesticides or herbicides in any of the residential areas. The leaves have a bitter, astringent quality that lingers on the palate.

A key component of SPFT's sustainability efforts is upholding a high degree of biodiversity. In order to join SPFT, prospective members must commit to growing at least ten kinds of crops. After witnessing how large corporations like Monsanto have wreaked havoc with Southeast Asian agricultural systems through the use of patented terminator seeds, SPFT steers clear of genetically modified crops altogether, fearful of losing control over another aspect of their livelihood to agribusiness. 'If you rely on genetically modified seeds, then you must always go back to the corporation for more,' Nittha tells me. As a safeguard, SPFT has been building a seed bank. 'When we visit grassroots movements in other regions we ask for their local seeds and distribute them to our members. The five communities within SPFT also exchange seeds.'

As we walk, Nittha points out pigs, ducks, cows, chickens and the former irrigation ditches left by Jiew Kang Jue Pattana where the farmers now raise tilapia and catfish. All of these resources are communal – the valuable herd of cattle is the closest thing the farmers have to a collective savings account. In order to raise money for larger expenses, including legal fees and organising costs for SPFT, members also sell a small number of cash products, including canned fermented bamboo shoots and flash-fried banana chips.

Over the past several years the farmers have invested in another commercial resource: they have started growing oil palm trees of their own, pooling the harvest of four communities and selling it through a cooperative. Since their oil

palms are still dwarfed by their towering counterparts across the dirt road, the cooperative collects a relatively modest haul. Nevertheless, they have high hopes of creating a more equitable model for the industry, one in which they are owners rather than employees. 'In our system, all of the profit goes back to community members. What we plan to do next is to provide a welfare system. We hope to be able to provide travel expenses for members to go to the hospital and for family to visit them,' Thonglue Yothapakdi, who runs the cooperative, tells me. More solemnly, he adds, 'We want to be able to provide burial expenses.'

Hundreds of hectares of oil palm plantations have been occupied by a palm oil company, forcing local farmers into hardship.

Near Klong Sai Pattana's central meeting hall is the memorial for the dead, a concrete obelisk topped with a steel coil and three stars – red, green and yellow. 'The red star is for the blood of the fallen workers, the green for the land, the yellow for virtue,' Surapol explains. 'The coiled spring is symbolic of a social evolution theory based on Marxism. Each rotation of the coil builds on top of the previous ones; it doesn't come back to the same origin.' At 7 a.m. members of the community gather around the statue, as they do every morning, to pay their respects and dance. Slowly they begin to clap, before breaking into song in one unified voice. They sing workers' songs of solidarity, of overcoming, all while swinging arthritic knees and joints. The scene resembles an aerobics class crossed with a Pentecostal revival service. 'This statue reminds us that the people who have fallen are still protecting land for those who are living,' Surapol says. 'Even if their physical bodies are gone, the spirit of their sacrifice continues. Even though they are dead, they continue to inspire the ideology of the next generation.'

When I meet Surapol for the last time, early on our final morning in Klong Sai Pattana, the sky is pale, the air thick with the promise of rain. He places a moka pot on a gas canister, and we both wait for the smell of coffee. 'In the past there were other farmers and community leaders who were murdered because of the work that they do,' Surapol says, his voice flat and hard. 'There was often no systematic documentation and records of what happened to them, but they are a part of our history and a part of how our society has evolved.'

Surapol has spent years trying to track down the families or the stories of some of the victims, often without success. For the most part the government has done little to acknowledge that atrocities such as the Red Drum Murders ever occurred. Surapol remembers a time when he fell into despair, when he was ready to abandon the idea that anything could ever change. Then in 2004 a trip to Brazil to visit the leaders of the Movimento dos Trabalhadores Rurais Sem Terra (MST, the Landless Workers' Movement) changed his mind. He left with a deep conviction about the

'For the most part the government has done little to acknowledge that atrocities such as the Red Drum Murders ever occurred.'

importance of creating pragmatic solutions and records so that the names of the dead would never again be erased. 'What is most impressive about the MST movement is that they had transformed these abstract theories into practice,' Surapol says. So he set about learning the tactics of non-violent resistance – how to choose your words when speaking out against authority, how to form alliances with other advocacy groups, how to stand united when your adversaries come for you.

The result of all those years of study is an effective organisational network that has survived in the face of seemingly insurmountable odds through a campaign of global outreach. SPFT has made sure that this time it will be harder to forget the names of those they have lost. Despite the efforts of the Thai government to shut it down, an exhibition titled *For Those Who Died Trying* by photographer Luke Duggleby features the portraits of Chai Boonthonglek and Klong Sai Pattana's other murdered land rights defenders and has travelled to the UN headquarters in Geneva as well as all around Thailand. Noting that revolution and systemic change in Thailand, from the 1970s to the pro-democracy protests of more recent times, has almost always begun with the country's youth, Surapol takes heart in the fact that thousands of students have shown their solidarity at peaceful protests. 'You know, in Christianity they believe that after you die you live happily in a fertile garden,' Surapol says. 'We believe that you can have that in this life if you join the struggle for land. You don't have to wait until after death.'

SPFT's struggle is far from over, but a turning point may be within reach. On 19 March 2021, after eight years of awaiting a verdict, the Thai Administrative Court sided with the farmers of Santi Pattana and ordered the Department of Land to remove United Palm Oil Industry Public from the land it unlawfully occupied. While this does not guarantee the long-term security of the community, it gives them the right to remain for now and ensures that both the people of Santi Pattana and SPFT's other communities will have a stronger standing in future court cases. After thirteen long years, the dream that drew so many people to this land no longer felt impossible.

*

Usa Suwannaphat did not attend the morning exercises on the last day of my stay, so after the crowd dispersed we returned to her house later in the morning to pay her a final visit. Although she tries to go every morning, sometimes her diabetes and blood pressure get the better of her. When she awoke she felt

Farmers deliver oil palm fruit to the wholesale market near Klong Sai Pattana.

A monument to four villagers – Somporn Patanapoom, Montha Chukaew, Pranee Bunrak and Chai Boonthonglek – killed on a community farm in Klong Sai Pattana while defending their land.

168 THE PASSENGER Diana Hubbell

Yupha Chuenbudh tearfully recounts how she and her community were harassed by the local mafia. She said, 'I am not afraid, and I will not move away. I will stand up and fight for our land.'

dizzy and decided to stay home, sitting on her porch beside several dozen papaya seedlings she had just finished planting. 'If I can plant at least five trees today I will be satisfied. I want to be able to grow something every day,' she says.

Usa's knotted fingers clutched the only photograph of her late husband that she owns. It's a blown-up ID portrait set on a backdrop of hard cerulean in a chipped gold-painted frame. The face inside is solemn, the features too low resolution to betray any hint of personality. But Usa remembers Chai's happiness when he tended to their rows of jackfruit trees, lemongrass and bird's-eye chillies. 'Chai loved this place,' she says. 'He planned that we would grow old here, peacefully and quietly, just me and him in this small house.'

Usa says that after Chai's death her daughter and the other members of Klong Sai Pattana were what kept her going. Maintaining the garden by herself becomes more of a challenge with each passing year, but she could not imagine going anywhere else. 'For us elderly people in Klong Sai Pattana, sometimes it's hard to keep fighting. Our knees don't always cooperate,' Usa says with a smile. 'I am not strong enough to do all of the work that Loong Chai used to do. I'm getting old. I am tired, but I am not going to give up.'

A display of Boys' Love novels at the Jamclub Book Store & Cafe, run by the publisher Jamsai, in Bangkok.

Boys' Love

In one of the Asian countries most open to LGBTQ+ themes, the Japanese genre of *yaoi* has flourished, with its love stories featuring gay men and aimed at a mainly heterosexual audience of young women. But, in spite of the global success of Thai TV series based on these books, many questions still remain over the way LGBTQ+ people's lives are represented.

JIDANUN LUEANGPIANSAMUT
Translated by Peera Songkünnatham

In 2017 I was awarded Thailand's biggest literary prize, at the time the youngest writer ever to have won the award. Following this, I was interviewed on a number of occasions, but what the media was most interested in wasn't the political, philosophical, dystopian fiction that I had written but my other work. I had revealed that I also wrote books about love between men, and that's what they all wanted to know more about and to discuss gender and sexuality. Journalists from forward-thinking media houses tended to be fairly well informed already, while those from more conservative organisations seemed still to be confused about any number of issues. Nonetheless, they were all respectful and listened closely to what I had to say.

Not long after that the international profile of LGBTQ+ novel series from Thailand grew so much that they started to grab global attention, and Thai media became better informed, so fewer questions about LGBTQ+ fiction or *yaoi* works came my way during interviews. At the same time that these novels began to travel abroad, so did I, and those same questions concerning LGBTQ+ fiction and gender fluidity in Thailand returned when I was interviewed by journalists in other countries. It seems that my writing life will be forever linked to such questions. Not that it bothers me – in fact, I enjoy talking about such topics. With each passing year the story around gender fluidity in society and in the literary sphere becomes increasingly complex, diverse and vibrant. There is a much better understanding and acceptance of gender and sexual equality – all of which is encouraging. Getting to tell that story and foster understanding between people is an honour for me.

In order to discuss LGBTQ+ literature in Thailand we need to refer back to other topics and define a number of terms. Ours is a time of contested definitions. Whoever determines the meaning of a word in either a positive or negative way will have the upper hand in any debate over a given social issue. Therefore the definitions and origins of relevant terms are important if we want to understand the big picture of the Thai LGBTQ+ literary scene more clearly. I run the risk of making this sound like a glossary in a dissertation, but believe me when I say that many contemporary debates wouldn't be so intractable if we paid more attention to defining

JIDANUN LUEANGPIANSAMUT is a Thai writer, the author of more than twenty-five books in various genres, from science fiction to romance to LGBTQ+ literature, some of which have been translated into English, Japanese and Chinese. In 2017 she was the youngest ever winner of the Southeast Asian Writers award, for *Singto Nok Khok*, a collection of dystopian short stories. In 2022 she participated in the University of Iowa's International Writing Program.

'While the film industry was clearly moving in a positive direction, the LGBTQ+ literary scene in the 2000s remained underground.'

the terms and to their historical background.

THE REPRESENTATION OF LGBTQ+ LIFE IN THAI MEDIA UP TO 2000

The appearance of LGBTQ+ and gender-fluid characters in Thai literature goes way back to the time when it was still penned in metrical verse. One interesting example is *Inlarat Kham Chan*, written in 1913 by Phraya Sisunthonwohan (Phan Salak), which features a character who switches back and forth between male and female. As a woman the character has sexual relations with a male character, but once reverted to their male form the character has no memory of having been female. This story of gender and sexual fluidity is told in the manner of an ancient fairy tale involving magic and local deities, but it does not rank among the best known from the period and nor is it generally classed as LGBTQ+ literature.

A more recent example would be a 1988 novel, a time when the baby-boomer generation was well into adulthood. At that point Thai society was not very accepting of LGBTQ+ people. Many found themselves forced into marriage by family or had to keep their true gender or sexuality a secret. Literary works from the period – for example *Baimai Thi Plitpliu* by Thommayanti – reflect society's intolerance at a time when being LGBTQ+ was considered a mental disorder and the lives of LGBTQ+ people as inherently unhappy, ones that would often end in tragedy, be it from unrequited love or suicide. Portrayals of LGBTQ+ characters at the time reflected contemporary social attitudes, and there wasn't much of a Thai readership for LGBTQ+ literature.

Things changed in the years between 1988 and 2000, however, and LGBTQ+ characters started to appear, often as comic relief. Many films of the period told LGBTQ+ stories that, as much as their plots attempted to build sympathy for or positive views towards LGBTQ+ characters, mainly fell back on displays of camp mannerisms and wisecracking. The community began to demand stories that showed other aspects of who they were, not just playing the clown. From 2007 onwards a new trend began to emerge in Thai films after Chukiat Sakveerakul created the teen romance *Love of Siam*, which tackled LGBTQ+ issues in an unprecedented manner through a coming-of-age story intertwined with the tale of a missing family member. That same year Poj Arnon released the film *Bangkok Love Story*, a drama about gay male life – albeit perhaps a rather heavy-handedly erotic portrayal of it – that was nonetheless one of the first commercial Thai films to be openly advertised as being a same-sex love story.

While the film industry was clearly moving in a positive direction, the LGBTQ+ literary scene in the 2000s remained underground. What was going on back then? Before we get to the answer, let us first define what is meant by *yaoi* and LGBTQ+ literature.

THE THIRD GENDER

At the age of sixteen Nong Toom became a Muay Thai star. The late 1990s was a time of crisis for Thai boxing, and the victories notched up by the long-haired, made-up teenager – who would give her defeated opponent a kiss at the end of each bout – helped put the sport back on track. Toom is a *kathoey*, a Thai term that originally described intersex people and now refers broadly to transvestite men, trans women and effeminate gay men. There is no satisfactory translation: some consider 'ladyboy' insulting, while the term transgender is an import from the West that fails to reflect the concept of a third gender with which most *kathoey* identify. Toom's story was made into a film (Ekachai Uekrongtham's *Beautiful Boxer*, 2003) but is only one of the many stories that reflect the relative openness of Thai society to *kathoey* – from the Iron Ladies who won the national men's volleyball championship in 1996 to the annual transgender beauty contest Miss Tiffany's Universe – but the reality is that gender fluidity is more tolerated than accepted. Many *kathoey* suffer discrimination within their families, at school, in terms of access to public services (the law does not allow you to change the sex assigned to you at birth on your documents, even if you have surgery) and in the workplace, which forces them to look for precarious jobs in the entertainment industry – perhaps one of the reasons for their visibility – and prostitution.

THE WORLD OF YAOI

The *yaoi* genre, which originated in Japan, focuses on stories of love between two gorgeous male characters. In its early days *yaoi* appeared in manga aimed at young girls, and both the creators and the readership were predominantly women. Early stories focused on the romantic or erotic interactions between the characters without paying too much attention to plot. Sometimes the stories were adaptations of previously published works. An example might be if readers reimagined the story in an adventure comic about a brave swordsman on a quest to save a princess but have the hero fall in love with a wizard in his entourage instead of the princess. Male characters and their sidekicks in novels tended to be reworked in this way by *yaoi* readers. These extended works are known as fanfiction, or, if in manga form, *dojinshi*, and examples familiar to Westerners might include Sherlock Holmes and Dr Watson, Batman and Robin, Captain Kirk and Mr Spock from *Star Trek*. In more recent times *yaoi* literature no longer limits itself to love scenes but has developed greater plot diversity, borrowing genre tropes from detective fiction, fantasy, drama or romantic comedy. Many feature original characters rather than being adaptations of other stories, although derivative *yaoi* works are still common, especially when it comes to characters based on movies, novels, comics or – a popular trend as of late – real-life celebrities such as well-known actors or K-pop stars.

I came to the *yaoi* community through reading Japanese manga, and this led to my discovery of *yaoi*. I liked it, and I have been reading and writing *yaoi* fiction ever since. *Yaoi* writers of my generation generally started in

Above: Celebrating gender diversity in Bangkok during Pride Month in Thailand.
Below: Thailand legalises same-sex marriage.

Boys' Love 175

one of two ways, either through their love of Japanese manga or by following K-pop boy bands. Once they witnessed the culture of 'shipping' – in which fans encourage male singers or other celebrities to couple up – they became drawn into the culture of *yaoi* literature.

A genre closely related to *yaoi* is Boys' Love, or BL, a term that is today used interchangeably with *yaoi*. Early *yaoi* and BL works focused on idealised romantic love – of a kind that did not truly reflect the struggles experienced by LGBTQ+ people – and were mostly read by a niche audience of young girls. LGBTQ+ readers, in contrast, tended to prefer Western MxM (male–male) fiction, which many believe reflects actual LGBTQ+ life more accurately than Eastern *yaoi* or BL.

At the time, the primarily young female readership of *yaoi* in Thailand weren't particularly interested in the fight for LGBTQ+ rights. *Yaoi* manuscripts were still not accepted by mainstream publishers, so the vast majority were self-published and sold by mail order to those in the know. In 2005 the underground nature of *yaoi* was exacerbated when an exposé of the genre was aired on television, characterising it as an obscene form that corrupted young people, and *yaoi* readers were forced to remain hidden for fear of social backlash. Girls who read *yaoi* or BL fiction could not talk about it openly online and had to retreat to members-only web forums. And yet this was happening at a time when *Love of Siam* and *Bangkok Love Story* were showing in cinemas nationwide.

The programme that 'exposed' *yaoi* was called *Raikan Loom Dum* ('The Black Hole Show'), which led *yaoi* readers over the age of thirty – and who had to remain guarded about their literary preferences – to dub the years around 2005 'the black hole era', which conveyed just how underground *yaoi* fiction was and how hard it was to get hold of. This is all but unknown to many Generation-Z *yaoi* readers, since by 2015 *Raikan Loom Dum* had been largely forgotten and much of the social stigma surrounding *yaoi* fiction had eased. Most *yaoi* and BL novels were at the time still self-published and largely sold by mail order, and, while ticketed events in conference rooms were also organised to sell the books directly to fans, the community remained a subculture.

The rise of Facebook allowed *yaoi* readers to move away from closed web forums to Facebook groups and to open conversations on the internet, and the number of readers steadily grew as a result. The market became so lucrative that major Thai publishing houses began to get in on the act and started publishing and distributing *yaoi* and BL fiction to be sold openly in bookshops nationwide.

Between 2017 and 2018 – as a newly crowned literary prizewinner – I went into a number of schools to give lectures as a serious, highbrow writer – but, as it turned out, the students were far more interested in my *yaoi* fiction than in my award-winning work. The number of girls who showed up to a literary presentation astounded their teachers. It was then that I first encountered *yaoi* readers who were assigned male at birth

Sirisak Chaited, aka Ton, a gender-diversity activist, reflects on gender equality for all, including those in religious communities. Ton attends every demonstration to demand political change.

(AMAB) – although the numbers were still small. Male gay writers also began to join the *yaoi* ranks, and today many AMAB readers and writers are part of the *yaoi* community, unlike the early days of exclusively female readership.

This opening out of the community, along with the involvement of LGBTQ+ readers and writers, has blurred the lines between *yaoi*, written for and read by women, and MxM, with its portrayals of more realistic representations of LGBTQ+ life. Younger Generation-Z readers began to demand that *yaoi* authors take a more socially responsible position by weaving the real-life problems and oppression suffered by LGBTQ+ people into their stories. Consequently, *yaoi* fiction has moved away from an exclusive focus on romantic love to a more expansive view of LGBTQ+ life, and the line between MxM and *yaoi* has become much less defined. Now it is commonplace to see both genres referenced under the umbrella term of LGBTQ+ fiction.

SUCCESS ABROAD AND GROWTH AT HOME

With the increasing popularity of *yaoi* novels, the television industry stepped into the market. Several TV production companies began making LGBTQ+-themed series, and the popularity and international reach of some of these exceeded all expectations. It began with *SOTUS* in 2016, followed by *Theory of Love* in 2019 and the hugely successful *Together* in 2020, and, ever since, all eyes have been on Thai television series. Thai *yaoi* literature has now been translated into Chinese (traditional characters), Japanese and English, and unofficial versions have also been translated into Spanish and Russian by fans who were

MORE (LGBTQ+) ROMANCE FOR ALL!

While *yaoi* is a niche genre in the West, it cannot be denied that the international literary scene is opening up to LGBTQ+ love stories. Romance and queer novels, which had long been the domain of a few small publishing houses, have benefited from the internet and self-publishing platforms like Wattpad. When the big publishers spotted the potential (2011 was the year of *Fifty Shades of Grey*, which originated as fanfiction), the genre moved on to paper and then ebooks, a medium that makes it possible to keep costs down while keeping up with the tastes of readers used to the flexibility of online content. Among these projects is the queer romance collection Carina Adores, released by North American romance publisher Harlequin (which has a similar output to Mills and Boon in some other anglophone territories). Between 2022 and 2023 sales of LGBTQ+ romance in the USA grew by 40 per cent, but the trend has been in evidence since 2016, reflecting a cultural shift. Romance has gone mainstream, and LGBTQ+ stories are reaching a broader audience of younger people with fewer prejudices: queer love stories such as Casey McQuiston's *Red, White & Royal Blue* are becoming bestsellers and giving rise to films and TV series. Then there is the TikTok effect whereby even older books such as Madeline Miller's *Song of Achilles* can start to trend several years after original publication. Based on the love story between Patroclus and Achilles, it was first published in 2011 and, following a TikTok appearance, found itself in the bestseller lists in 2021 with millions of copies sold.

BLAZING A TRAIL

It was 18 June 2024, and rainbow flags were flying in the streets of Bangkok as people danced and sang. Not for Pride, which had been held earlier in the month, but to celebrate the Thai senate's approval of the bill on same-sex marriage, following the lower house's approval in March. To be exact, it was a modification to an existing law, replacing 'woman' and 'man' with neutral terms and describing marriage as an agreement between two people. The king's approval, which is needed for any law to come into force, was taken as read, given the country's widespread support for equal marriage – 60 per cent of the population, according to a survey by the Pew Research Center – reflecting a tolerant attitude even among religious representatives. The first weddings took place in January 2025, with partners now enjoying all the same rights previously granted only to heterosexual couples, including those relating to inheritance and adoption.
So Thailand has become the first country in Southeast Asia and the third in Asia (after Taiwan and Nepal) to extend the right to marry to all couples, giving hope to LGBTQ+ people right across the region. The road that led to this historic day was neither easy nor short, however – the first proposed law dates back to 2012 – and it doesn't mean that the fight is over. On some issues Thailand remains a conservative country; in February 2024 a proposal was rejected that would have allowed trans people to change gender on their official documents.

unable to acquire translation rights officially but who asked for permission to translate and put them online so readers in their own languages could enjoy the work. Copyright concerns aside, this is proof of international interest in Thai *yaoi* fiction.

Not much Thai literature of any kind has been translated into foreign languages in the past, so the international success of Thai LGBTQ+ fiction is an important step forward. In 2024 the Thailand booth at the Taipei International Book Exhibition invited novelists on to a panel discussion that focused on *yaoi*/LGBTQ+ literature; the event was extremely well attended by Taiwanese readers. Many media outlets approached the authors for interviews, and television producers also reached out to purchase the rights to adapt a number of novels into series. This was a significant milestone for Thai literature, something that had never been achieved before.

Domestically, social acceptance has also grown enormously, with powerful political figures all espousing positivity with regard to the popularity of LGBTQ+ media. Pita Limjaroenrat, for example – the prime ministerial candidate whose party won the most votes in the 2023 general elections – attended the premiere of *Man Suang* (2023), an LGBTQ+ film with a political subtext. Limjaroenrat represented a new-generation political party, the Move Forward Party, which became a key player in Thai politics for a few years. It had a progressive agenda with a younger supporter base and was involved in the political protests of 2020. These demonstrations ran alongside campaigns by LGBTQ+ communities and feminist groups, campaigns which have led to Pride parades, a push for the legalisation of same-sex marriage

Above: Posters of popular Boys' Love novels series, some of which have been adapted for film and TV.
Below: The reading corner of the Jamclub Book Store & Cafe.

(which was finally passed into law in 2024) and a broader acceptance of the diverse nature of gender and sexuality.

This social phenomenon nudged an already considerably LGBTQ+-friendly society further towards the acceptance of gender and sexual fluidity. Generation X and the generations that followed all now embrace this, while most baby boomers are generally accepting of LGBTQ+ people in the media or in society – although they might still have concerns about their own children or grandchildren coming out as LGBTQ+. It remains to be seen whether, in ten years' time when their own children and grandchildren grow into adults, Generations X and Y will be as accepting of LGBTQ+ people in their own families as they now say they are of those in the media.

QUESTIONS STILL TO BE RESOLVED

Those in the LGBTQ+ literary community are often one step ahead of wider society when it comes to discussions about gender, so in the past, when gender and sexual diversity were still taboo topics for much of society, *yaoi* readers generally held more positive views. Now that Thai society is broadly positive towards LGBTQ+ individuals, the *yaoi* fiction community is engaging in deeper debates about gender.

One hot topic is that of the theme of romantic love in *yaoi* fiction, and how the genre fails to reflect the real problems and social pressures faced by LGBTQ+ people. Many readers are calling for *yaoi* authors to incorporate these elements into their stories and not focus solely on romance. Consequently, *yaoi* authors are now weaving social issues into their stories. However, works currently available in translation tend to date back at least five years from original publication in Thailand, meaning they may have been written before such matters were taken into account. When I was in Taiwan I heard readers raising questions about the lack of engagement with social issues in Thai *yaoi*. In response, the authors pointed out that newer novels did address these questions more, that romance was no longer their sole focus but that foreign readers might just have to wait a couple of years to be able to read the more recent books.

Still, there are ways in which *yaoi* fiction and LGBTQ+ life do diverge. One example is that *yaoi* fiction clearly distinguishes who is the 'male' in the relationship from the 'female', even though LGBTQ+ people may be flexible in their sexual and gender roles. Most writers, however, continue to fall back on the gender-binary model in characterising relationships, and many readers remain very attached to this. Thai *yaoi* fiction tends to refer to the LGBTQ+ couple as 'husband and wife', but during the course of the three months I spent in Taipei I met several Taiwanese readers of Thai fiction who took issue with this because in their view a gay male couple ought to be 'husband and husband'. A Thai writer friend of mine answered that Thai *yaoi* novels were increasingly doing this.

But it's not only Taiwanese readers who raise the issue; readers in Thailand have long discussed the imposition of the gender-binary model on the makeup and behaviour of characters. For example, one of the protagonists will often be portrayed as strong, muscular and tall, while the other must be slight and light-skinned with feminine facial features, which some readers interpret as an attempt to impose heterosexual norms

> 'A large number of readers love novels with this kind of binary framework. This has led to a boom in works set in fantasy universes where a male protagonist can fall pregnant.'

on homosexual couples. Despite the long-running debates within the community, this topic has never died away because a large number of readers love novels with this kind of binary framework. This has led to a boom in works set in fantasy universes where a male protagonist can fall pregnant, assume the role of a mother, know the pain of giving birth and cradle and breastfeed their baby. Amid criticism over its appropriateness, the mpreg (male pregnancy) genre regularly features in the best-seller lists. It is undeniable that, however progressive the gender discourse on social media might be, plenty of readers continue to enjoy reading and buying novels dubbed 'problematic' by progressives.

A further issue is just how heated the arguments on social media have become. If a reader were to browse the shelves of heterosexual romance novels, some of which have been there for decades, they would probably find examples of twisted relationships – a love that blossoms despite the male

protagonist having raped the female protagonist or a relationship that borders on paedophilia, for example. These traits appear in *yaoi* novels, too, but in this current decade, both heterosexual and LGBTQ+ novels feature them far less following recent culture shifts. *Yaoi* writers are moving away from such elements in favour of more positive stories. However, those who write in this vein or who had works of this nature published in the past can face harsh criticism on social media and can even be boycotted. The attacks go way beyond mere criticism and descend into condemnation and abusive language, which leads many writers to self-censor constantly to protect themselves from online hate. As this intensifies, more people are beginning to express their exasperation with the new culture, with some even turning to oppressive and anti-egalitarian ideologies in trying to find allies when they come under attack.

I worry about this because, while progressives set out on their campaigns with good intentions, their actions might have the opposite effect of pushing people towards supporting older patriarchal beliefs instead, which I doubt most people want. These internet spats can turn so nasty that they escalate into hatred without fostering any sympathy or understanding among people. I hope that in the future people will find more ways to meet in the middle so that each can express their viewpoint without tipping over into hate or causing harm to other parties – who are, after all, actual humans behind the computer screen.

AN IMMINENT NEW WAVE

If you've reached this point you might be wondering whether LGBTQ+ literature in Thailand consists only of Boys' Love stories. In fact, going right back to the early days of *yaoi*, another genre emerged alongside it to tell stories about love between women, *yuri*, which, like *yaoi*, has a complex subculture of its own. Recently some in the community have been demanding that the term 'sapphic' be used in place of *yuri* because it is seen as more inclusive. Nevertheless, I will stick with *yuri* for the purposes of this article, as it corresponds to the use of *yaoi*.

Interestingly, while *yuri* in Japan is marketed to male readers – much as *yaoi* in its early days was marketed to a female readership – in Thailand the publishers, writers and readers of *yuri* fiction are not men but women, lesbian and otherwise. The Thai *yuri* readership is comprised of new-generation feminists who are passionate about gender equality and politics.

Yuri used to have a rather small audience in Thailand, but the numbers have steadily risen in recent years, even though its share is still lower than that of *yaoi*. In 2023, when talking to a number of television production companies, I learned that they were at saturation point for *yaoi* series and were now showing an interest in *yuri*. It is likely that within a year or two a *yuri* wave will thrive in Thailand, and soon Thai lesbian series will gain global attention in the same way as the popular Thai gay series have in the past. 🖋

Ethnotourism

'Giraffe Women' and the Commodification of Minorities

ANDREA STAID
Translated by Alan Thawley

It was 2018, and I was making yet another foray into the sinuous roads that cut through the mountains of Northern Thailand. In a decade of travelling through Thailand, Laos, Myanmar and Vietnam I had already witnessed the travel agencies' increasing interest in 'ethnic minorities', a phenomenon that is growing at pace. Ready-made packages offered in big cities such as Bangkok promise curious travellers from all around the world the opportunity to immerse themselves in 'authentic' experiences and come into contact with the Indigenous peoples who inhabit the mountainous areas of the North. A meeting, on paper, between two diametrically opposed worlds; an opportunity to experience ancient traditions and customs.

But behind this promise of exoticism and discovery, often questionable in itself, lies a much grimmer reality. Ethnic minorities now find themselves transformed into something to be exhibited, tourist attractions to be consumed like souvenirs, their cultures

trivialised and reduced to picturesque folklore to satisfy Western travellers' thirst for adventure.

A striking example is that of the Kayan, aka the Padaung, who currently live in central-eastern Myanmar and the northwestern areas of Thailand and are best known for the iconic metal ring necklaces worn by the women, who are called 'giraffe women' as a result. During a visit to their villages I was dismayed by the incessant flow of tourists from every corner of the globe. They arrived in taxis, buses and minibuses, driven by the desire to immortalise these anthropological 'oddities' in their photographs. Customs, rituals, festivals and arts: a rich and precious cultural heritage reduced to a mere service to be consumed by visitors.

This is the fate of the Kayan, victims of ethnotourism that all too often turns into exploitation and commodification – an exploitation that mainly targets the women because the men, with no unusual body modification, hold no interest for the visitors. The women, who are the main attraction in their villages, receive a meagre salary from the government ranging between 1,500 and 2,000 baht ($45–60) a month. But this is not their only source of income: posing for photographs and selling textiles and handicrafts supplement the

ANDREA STAID is an Italian anthropologist, writer and researcher whose work revolves around the core philosophy that humans and nature are indivisible. Through his writings he advocates for rethinking the way we conceive our relationship with nature to be able to conceive new models of inhabiting the Earth. He currently manages the anthropology series for the publisher Meltemi and is a professor at the Nuova Accademia di Belle Arti in Milan and at the University of Genoa. His publications have been translated into Greek, German, Spanish, Chinese and Portuguese. His most recent book is *Essere natura* ('Being Nature', 2022).

family budget. Whether they are old or young, there is little difference in their situation, except that the former receive slightly higher salaries and the latter have to attend school and therefore earn less. In any case, the salary disappears in the low season, leaving families to face their difficulties with no support apart from the rice, salt and oil supplied in limited quantities by local NGOs.

    The lives of the Kayan people were turned upside down by their arrival in Thailand between the late 1980s and late 1990s; they were seeking a safe refuge and could not have imagined that they would become a tourist attraction to be exploited. Local authorities have imposed specific laws on these communities, prohibiting them from raising animals, hunting and owning or cultivating land, restrictions that severely impact their autonomy and their traditional lifestyle, compelling them to accept this involuntary commodification. Many Kayan, having fled civil wars and oppressive regimes in neighbouring countries, particularly Myanmar, now find themselves the victims of ruthless economic interests linked to tourism. Transformed into fairground attractions, like animals in a human zoo, they are forced to see their culture debased. Deprived of their freedom of choice, they are hanging by a slender thread, the tourist industry upon which their survival depends.

Kayan women in particular are victims of a dual oppression. Their main activity, regardless of their age, is to sit in public areas of the village, ready to pose for photos or sell souvenirs to tourists – 'ethnic' models paid by visitors per photograph. Their earnings are the main source of income for their families, and this has led to the worrying trend of parents encouraging their daughters to wear the rings from a young age. Traditionally, only a limited number of women in each community would adorn themselves this way, but with the arrival of tourism the demand is growing as is the number of girls forced to undergo the painful process of stretching their necks. Tradition required lengthy timeframes for this rite of initiation, but the tourist industry, with its thirst for profit, has accelerated the process – the greatest suffering falls upon these young women. The Thai authorities, cynically, present this choice as beneficial for the Kayan, painting an idyllic picture of the tourist sector improving their lives. They encourage visits to the villages, transforming them into living museums where culture becomes a spectacle.

I believe a change of direction is needed to a form of tourism based on respect, the valuing of local cultures and protecting the rights of Indigenous peoples. These issues have been hotly debated in Thailand as well, from as far back as 1997 when the alarm was sounded by Poonsak Sunthornpanikit, president of the Mae Hong Son chamber of commerce, that the reduction of the Kayan groups, famous for their characteristic neck rings, to a mere tourist commodity was a clear violation of their human rights. We need to imagine a form of tourism that acts as a bridge for knowledge and growth rather than a weapon for exploitation and commodification. This is the only way that we can ensure a dignified future for the Kayan and all the peoples who live in the mountains of Northern Thailand.

Ethnotourism

The Playlist

You can listen to this playlist at:
open.spotify.com/user/iperborea

'TED' YUTHANA BOONORM
Translated by Peera Songkünnatham

If you are familiar with the flavours of Thai food, you can probably guess what Thai music might taste like: spicy, sweet, sour and salty. It can be hot or cold. If Thai food is to your taste, it won't be hard for you to find Thai artists that you'll like, so here's my selection of twelve Thai songs that give some idea of the diversity found in Thai music today.

'Thattong Sound' by Youngohm ft. Sonofo and 'Hey Hey' by Milli and Hi Arpaporn are representative recent Thai-style hits. They blend modern beats with Thai dance rhythms and combine them with rap, which is the idiom in which Thai youth expresses itself. These two songs will give you a window on what's going on in the country now. Three Man Down and Tattoo Colour are the two most important artists at the moment, and their names appear on posters for every music festival. Representing a new generation of talented pop idols are Jeff Satur, Ink Waruntorn and Pixxie. Jeff writes and produces his own work, Ink is a classically trained singer and Pixxie excels both as a dancer and a singer. With Joey Phuwasit and Taitosmith we dive into the kind of authentic Thai music that no Thai can do without, a mix of rock and regional folk in songs that reflect the lives of the rural working class. Phum, HYBS and Tilly Birds represent the Thai sounds that broke out to find fans right across Asia.

While twelve songs cannot fully encompass the range of contemporary Thai music, these should be a good place to start your exploration. Enjoy the adventure.

'TED' YUTHANA BOONORM is a veteran of the Thai music industry, in which, for more than thirty years, he has worked as a producer, commentator and judge at music competitions as well as a radio DJ. He is the founder of the Big Mountain Music Festival, the largest music festival in Thailand.

1
Thattong Sound
Youngohm
ft. Sonofo
2023

2
Hey Hey
Milli
and Hi
Arpaporn
2024

3
Broken Clock
Three Man
Down
2023

4
SuperCarCare
Tattoo Colour
and D Gerrard
2022

5
Fade
Jeff Satur
2024

6
Eyes Don't Lie
Ink Waruntorn
2022

7
Rain
Pixxie
2023

8
นะหน้าทอง
Joey
Phuwasit
2022

9
เพื่อชีวิตกู
Taitosmith
2022

10
Lover Boy
Phum
Viphurit
2018

11
*Dancing
with My Phone*
HYBS
2022

12
Same Page?
Tilly Birds
2020

The Playlist

Digging Deeper

FICTION

Tew Bunnag
Naga's Journey
Orchid Press, 2007

Richard Flanagan
The Narrow Road to the Deep North
Vintage, 2015

Alex Garland
The Beach
Riverhead, 1998 (USA) / (reprint edition) Penguin, 2017 (UK)

Uthis Haemamool
The Fabulist
Penguin Random House, 2023

Rattawut Lapcharoensap
Sightseeing
Grove Press, 2007 (USA) /
Atlantic Books, 2006 (UK)

Emma Larkin
Comrade Aeon's Field Guide to Bangkok
Granta, 2022

Elisa Macellari
Papaya Salad
Dark Horse, 2020

Veeraporn Nitiprapha
*Memories of the Memories
of the Black Rose Cat*
River Books, 2022

Duanwad Pimwana
Bright
Two Lines Press, 2019

Saneh Sangsuk
The Understory
Deep Vellum, 2024 (USA) /
Peirene Press, 2023 (UK)

Claudio Sopranzetti, Sara Fabbri, Chiara Natalucci
The King of Bangkok
University of Toronto Press, 2021

Pitchaya Sudbanthad
Bangkok Wakes to Rain
Riverhead, 2019 (USA) / Sceptre, 2019 (UK)

Pira Sudham
Monsoon Country
(8th edition) DCO Books, 2022

Prabda Yoon
Moving Parts
Tilted Axis, 2018

NON-FICTION

Philip Cornwel-Smith
Very Bangkok: In the City of the Senses
River Books, 2020

Philip Cornwel-Smith
Very Thai: Everyday Popular Culture
(2nd revised edition) River Books, 2022

Jerry Hopkins
*Bangkok Babylon: The Real-Life Exploits
of Bangkok's Legendary Expatriates
Are Often Stranger Than Fiction*
Tuttle Publishing, 2009

Rupert Mann
Bangkok Street Art and Graffiti: Hope Full, Hope Less, Hope Well
River Books, 2022

Martino Nicoletti
The Zoo of the Giraffe Women: A Journey Among the Kayan of Northern Thailand
Éditions le Loup des Steppes, 2015

Lawrence Osborne
Bangkok Days
North Point Press, 2009 (USA) / Vintage, 2010 (UK)

Nicolas Verstappen
The Art of Thai Comics: A Century of Strips and Stripes
River Books, 2022

Upasika Kee Nanayon
Pure and Simple
Wisdom Publications, 2005

FILM AND TV

Lee Chatametikool
Concrete Clouds
2013

Kongdej Jaturanrasamee
Midnight My Love
2005

Ekalak Klunson
RedLife
2023

Sitisiri Mongkolsiri
Hunger
2023

Prempapat Plittapolkranpim
The Last Breath of Sam Yan
2023

Pen-Ek Ratanaruang
Last Life in the Universe
2003

Chookiat Sakveerakul
Love of Siam
2007

Wisit Sasanatieng
Citizen Dog
2004

Tom Shankland, Hans Herbots
The Serpent
2021

Adisorn Tresirikasem
Bangkok Traffic (Love) Story
2009

Kittichai Wanprasert
Hurts Like Hell
2022

Apichatpong Weerasethakul
Tropical Malady
2004

Graphic design and art direction: Tomo Tomo and Pietro Buffa

Photography: Jittrapon Kaicome
Photographic content curated by Prospekt Photographers: Francesco Merlini with Michela Mosca
Illustrations: Edoardo Massa
Infographics and cartography: Propp

Managing editor (English-language edition): Simon Smith

Thanks to: Johny Adhikari, Peerapon Boonyakiat, Teeranet Chaisuwan, Narisa Chakrabongse, Wan Chantavilasvong, Tanat Chayaphattharitthee, Nalina Chayasombat, Gioia Guerzoni, Mai Janta, Sippachai Kunnuwong, Anwar Ismail MA IS, Massimo Morello, Lorenza Pignatti, Tommaso Pincio, Francesco Radicioni, Claudio Sopranzetti, Andrea Staid, Prabda Yoon

The opinions expressed in this publication are those of the authors and do not purport to reflect the views and opinions of the publishers. All content not specifically credited was written by The Passenger.

http://europaeditions.com/thepassenger
http://europaeditions.co.uk/thepassenger
#ThePassengerMag

The Passenger – Thailand © Iperborea S.r.l., Milan, and Europa Editions, 2025

Translators: Italian — Eleanor Chapman ('Expecto Patronum', 'Add a Pinch of Coriander', 'Call 112', *The Passenger* texts), Alan Thawley ('Ethnotourism', *The Passenger* texts); Thai — Noh Anothai ('The Deep South', 'A Country with No Refugees'), Peera Songkünnatham ('Boys' Love', 'The Playlist')

Translations © Iperborea S.r.l., Milan, and Europa Editions, 2025

ISBN 9781787705777

All Rights Reserved. No part of this publication may be reproduced, stored in a retrieval system or transmitted in any form or by any means without the written permission of the publishers and copyright owners.

The moral rights of the authors and other copyright-holders are hereby asserted in accordance with the Copyright Designs and Patents Act 1988.

Printed on Munken Pure thanks to the support of Arctic Paper Printed by ELCOGRAF S.p.A., Verona, Italy

The Song: 'Bangkok Legacy'
© Prabda Yoon, 2024

'Expecto Patronum'
© Claudio Sopranzetti, 2024

Becoming Bangkokian: How to Be a Hyphen-Thai
© Philip Cornwel-Smith, 2024. The article includes material first published in *Very Bangkok*, published by River Books, 2020.

Higher Powers
© Pitchaya Sudbanthad, 2024

Generational Trauma in the Deep South
© Veerapong Soontornchattrawat, 2024

Heartland
© Peera Songkünnatham, 2024

The Bodiless Woman and Other Ghost Stories
© Emma Larkin, 2024

Add a Pinch of Coriander
© Valeria Palermi, 2024

A Country With No Refugees
© Nicha Wachpanich, 2024

There Has Been Blood
© Diana Hubbell, 2021. First published in *Eater* in August 2021. The writing of this article was supported in part by a Pulitzer Traveling Fellowship.

Boys' Love
© Jidanun Lueangpiansamut, 2024

Ethnotourism
© Andrea Staid, 2024

The Playlist
© 'Ted' Yuthana Boonorm, 2024